DK EYEWITNESS

T0063860

TOP 10
PHUKET

Top 10 Phuket Highlights

The Top 10 of Everything

CONTENTS

Phuket Area by Area

Streetsmart

Within each Top 10 list in this book, no hierarchy of quality or popularity is implied. All 10 are, in the editor's opinion, of roughly equal merit.

Throughout this book, floors are referred to in accordance with American usage; i.e., the "first floor" is at ground level.

Title page, front cover and spine *The tranquil Cheuw Laan Lake, Khao Sok National Park* ***Back cover, clockwise from top left*** *Tom Yum soup with shrimp; province of Patong; Patong Beach; Cheow Laan Lake; Wat Chalong Temple*

The rapid rate at which the world is changing is constantly keeping the DK Eyewitness team on our toes. While we've worked hard to ensure that this edition of Phuket is accurate and up-to-date, we know that opening hours alter, standards shift, prices fluctuate, places close and new ones pop up in their stead. So, if you notice we've got something wrong or left something out, we want to hear about it. Please get in touch at **travelguides@dk.com**

Welcome to
Phuket

With pearly white sand beaches, ancient rainforests teeming with wildlife, and tranquil temples and shrines, Thailand's largest island offers a tropical getaway like no other, whether you're seeking a beach holiday, a cultural break or a hiking trip. With DK Eyewitness Top 10 Phuket, it is yours to explore.

Although many people come to Phuket (pronounced POO-get) to laze on its beaches, there's much to discover beyond the sand. Join the crowds in one of **Patong**'s bustling street markets, admire the 19th-century temple **Wat Chalong** and hop between restaurants and street food stalls in **Phuket Town**, before kicking back on lovely **Kata Beach**.

There's also much to see beyond this 50-mile- (80-km-) long island, which is connected to the mainland by a bridge and surrounded by smaller islands. The karst cliffs and sea caves of **Phang Nga Bay** are rivaled by the surging waterfalls in the rainforests of **Khao Sok National Park**, north of Phuket. The nearby **Similan Islands** are rated among the world's top ten diving sites, and **Ko Phi Phi Don**, a short boat ride south of Phuket, offers a heady mix of raucous parties and silent, secluded beaches.

Whether you're visiting for a weekend or a week, our Top 10 guide brings together the best of everything Phuket and the surrounding areas have to offer, from the world-class resorts lining **Mai Khao Beach** to the pristine rainforests of **Khao Phra Thaeo Royal Forest and Wildlife Reserve**. The guide gives you useful tips throughout, from seeking out what's free to places off the beaten path, alongside five easy-to-follow itineraries, designed to help you visit a clutch of sights in a short space of time. Add inspiring photography and detailed maps, and you've got the essential pocket-sized travel companion. **Enjoy the book, and enjoy Phuket**.

Clockwise from top: Colorful boats at James Bond Island in Phang Nga Bay, scuba diver in the Similan Islands, statue of the Buddha, stilt houses on Cheow Laan Lake, Chinese dragon carvings at Tha Rua shrine, junks in Phang Nga Bay, Sino-Portuguese buildings in Phuket

Exploring Phuket

While it is tempting to find your perfect beach and just relax there, Phuket offers an amazingly wide variety of treasures to discover. Beyond the beaches are rain forests, and the town of Phuket is an architectural and cultural jewel. To take in everything will require some form of private transport, but a good network of ferries serves the islands that surround Phuket. Here are two itineraries to help you make the most of your stay.

To Khao Sok
National Park
75 miles (120 km)

Mai Khao Beach

Sirinat
National Park

Phang Nga Bay, with its dramatic limestone pillars and aquatic grottoes, can be explored by traditional junk cruise, kayaking expedition, or long-tailed boat.

Patong Beach

Chal

Key
— Two-day itinerary
— Seven-day itinerary

Kata Beach

Phromthep
Cape

Two Days in Phuket

Day ❶
MORNING
Explore the streets of old **Phuket Town** (see pp12–15), admiring the Sino-Portuguese architecture, and visit one of the atmospheric old **Chinese shrines** (see pp44–5).
AFTERNOON
Head southwest from Phuket Town to **Wat Chalong** (see pp16–17), Phuket's most famous Buddhist temple. Drive to **Phromthep Cape** (see p48) and watch the sun set on the island's southern tip. Stay overnight at nearby **Kata Beach** (see pp28–9) or **Patong Beach** (see pp18–19) on the west coast.

Day ❷
MORNING
Drive to **Sirinat National Park** (see pp22–3) and stroll along the quiet and undeveloped Mai Khao Beach. There are simple beachside seafood stalls here, perfect for lunch.

AFTERNOON
Head to **Khao Phra Thaeo Royal Forest and Wildlife Reserve** (see pp20–21) via routes 402 and 4127. Trek to Ton Sai Waterfall for a swim, then visit the **Gibbon Rehabilitation Project**. Have dinner in **Phuket Town** (see pp12–15).

Seven Days in Phuket

Day ❶
Follow the morning's plan for Day 1 of the Phuket itinerary, taking in the sights of historic old **Phuket Town** (see pp12–15). After lunch, take a taxi to Rassada Port, then board a ferry to Ko Yao Noi in **Phang Nga Bay** (see pp36–7). Spend your first night here.

Day ❷
Take a boat tour of the dramatic limestone stacks and mangrove forests of the bay, then visit the amazing sea caves on a kayaking expedition in the evening. Spend a second night at Ko Yao Noi.

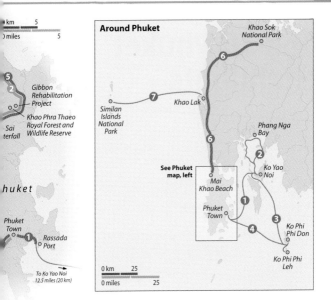

Day ❸
Take a boat from Ko Yao Noi to **Ko Phi Phi Don** (see p101) to spend a night there. Enjoy the stunning views from the **Phi Phi Viewpoint** (see p99), then leave the busy Tonsai area and follow the coast to **Ko Phi Phi Leh** (see p48), where you can swim and snorkel the evening away. This islet is uninhabited, but has been the set for several Hollywood movies.

Day ❹
Make your way back to Phuket by speedboat or ferry, and then follow the afternoon's plan for Day 1 of the Phuket itinerary.

Day ❺
Follow the program for Day 2 of the Phuket itinerary, but spend the night at **Mai Khao Beach** (see p23).

Day ❻
Spend the day kayaking or trekking in **Khao Sok National Park** (see pp32–5). This pristine rainforest environment includes spectacular limestone cliffs and a wide variety of flora and fauna. Stay overnight in the coastal town of **Khao Lak** (see p100). This is mainly a jumping off place for dive trips to the islands, but Nang Tong beach, just south of town, is lovely and quiet.

Day ❼
Take a boat tour to the **Similan Islands National Park** (see pp30–31), 50 miles (80 km) from **Khao Lak** (see p100). Both the scuba diving and snorkeling here are superb. Note that the islands are closed from mid-May to mid-October due to poor weather.

Phi Phi Viewpoint on Phi Phi Don offers views over two magnificent bays, Loh Dalum and Tonsai.

Top 10 Phuket Highlights

Ko Tapu karst formation at James
Bond Island, Phang Nga Bay

🔟 Phuket Highlights

Phuket's extraordinary tropical setting needs little introduction. The marvelous white-sand beaches, rolling green hills, and crystal-clear waters have lured visitors for centuries. But the island has more than sublime beaches. Phuket and its environs are also home to a multitude of cultural highlights.

Phuket Town ①
Magnificent architecture, Chinese shrines, bustling outdoor marketplaces, and delicious local dishes are all found in Phuket's cultural heart *(see pp12–15)*.

② Wat Chalong
Phuket's most important Buddhist temple is lavish with sacred sculptures and imagery. The Grand Pagoda houses a bone fragment of the Buddha himself *(see pp16–17)*.

Patong ③
Wild and uninhibited, Patong is the island's busiest tourist beach. Home to countless hotels, restaurants, and nightclubs, this is the ideal spot for people who want to be in the middle of the action *(see pp18–19)*.

④ Khao Phra Thaeo Royal Forest and Wildlife Reserve
With jungle trails, waterfalls, and many native animals and plants, this national park features a wealth of wild attractions *(see pp20–21)*.

Sirinat National Park ⑤
On Phuket's pristine northwest coast, Sirinat National Park grants protection to a large area of undeveloped beachfront, as well as the island's last surviving mangrove forest. A number of upscale hotels are located here *(see pp22–3)*.

Suan
Maphrao

Phuket

Sirinat
National Park ⑤

Sakoo

Nai
Thon

Bang
Tao Bay

Cherngtalay

Kamala
Bay

Kama

Patong ③

Karon

Kata Beach ⑦

Nai Harn ⑥
Beach

Around Phuket

Khao Sok National Park 9
Takua Pa
Thap Lamu
8 Similan Islands National Park
Phang Nga
Andaman Sea
Kok Loi
Phuket
10 Phang Nga Bay
Phuket Town

0 km 30
0 miles 30

Kung Bay
Muang Mai
Bang Rong
4 Khao Phra Thaeo Royal Forest and Wildlife Reserve
halang
Na Sat
Tha Rua
Sapam Bay
athu
Ratsada
1 Phuket Town
2 Wat Chalong
Ao Makham
Ao Chalong
Chalong Bay
awai

0 km 5
0 miles 5

6 Nai Harn Beach

At Phuket's southern tip, this idyllic beach provides one of the island's loveliest tropical backdrops. Phromthep Cape offers breathtaking sunset views *(see pp26–7)*.

7 Kata Beach

Once a hippie haven, Kata is now home to upscale resorts, and is a favorite with couples and families. The gorgeous beach and clear turquoise waters are highlights *(see pp28–9)*.

8 Similan Islands National Park

The waters surrounding the Similans provide incredible visibility, ideal for viewing colorful marine life and dramatic underwater rock formations and reefs. This is one of the world's top diving destinations *(see pp30–31)*.

9 Khao Sok National Park

At the heart of this park are ancient evergreen forests, majestic limestone peaks, and Cheow Laan Lake, with its floating bamboo-raft houses *(see pp32–5)*.

10 Phang Nga Bay

Stunning limestone cliffs jut up from this bay, where world-famous sights include James Bond Island and the magnificent Ko Phi Phi. Kayakers can explore the water tunnels, caves, and uninhabited islands *(see pp36–7)*.

10 ⭐ Phuket Town

The historical and administrative center of Phuket traces its roots back centuries – first to Indigenous tribes and later to the Chinese immigrants who arrived here during the 19th-century tin-mining boom. Today, Phuket Town continues to thrive as one of the island's most concentrated cultural areas, with architectural treasures, Chinese shrines, colorful markets, and restaurants that serve some of Phuket's most delicious local cuisines.

Ko Sirey ①

Linked to Phuket Town via a small bridge, Sirey Island features hilly forest trails that wind their way through rubber plantations. Perched on a hilltop, Ko Sirey temple **(right)** enjoys sea views and features a large reclining Buddha image in its main hall.

② Sunday Walking Street Market

Thalang Road closes to traffic from 4pm every Sunday for this colorful market **(above)**, which offers many locally made craft items, along with clothes and good food stalls. The historic buildings here are illuminated for the occasion.

③ Naka Weekend Market

Located close to the Nakaram Temple on Virat Hongyok Road, and near the Central Festival mall, this market is ideal for buying food, souvenirs, gifts, and clothing.

④ Marvelous Architecture

The distinctive style of architecture *(see pp14–15)* found in Phuket Town's old shop houses and mansions **(below)** is known as Sino-Portuguese. This highly attractive blend of Eastern and Western styles dates from the late 19th century.

Phuket Town

Kutu

Phuket Town 2 miles (3 km)

❼ ❻ ❾ ❺ ❷ ❶ ❸ ❽ ❿

7 Phuket Cultural Centre

Located on the Rajabhat University campus, this museum **(left)** houses old Thai shadow puppets, tin-mining artifacts, historic photographs, and books on local culture.

8 Suan Luang Park

This pleasant garden with lovely lotus ponds comes alive in the early mornings, when people come to exercise and perform Tai Chi.

ORIGINS OF THE VEGETARIAN FESTIVAL

In 1825, a traveling Chinese opera company in Kathu contracted malaria. According to legend, the afflicted nursed themselves back to health by following a strict vegetarian diet to purify their minds and bodies, and to honor the nine Emperor Gods of Chinese Taoism. After they recovered, the first Vegetarian Festival was held to thank the gods.

5 Chinese Shrines

Vibrant and colorful art can be admired at Chinese temples *(see pp44–5)* throughout the town. The shrines play an important role during the Chinese New Year and the annual Phuket Vegetarian Festival.

6 Monkey Hill

Although the views from atop nearby Rang Hill are more impressive, Monkey Hill offers a more unusual experience, as hordes of macaque monkeys congregate near the hilltop. Keep hold of your belongings – the monkeys may try to snatch them.

9 Rang Hill

Wonderful views of Phuket Town can be enjoyed from the summit of Rang Hill, where a breezy, tree-shaded park **(above)** also provides a relaxing venue for a picnic, some exercise, or simply reading a book.

10 Phuket Vegetarian Festival

This annual festival is held over nine days in late September/early October. Some devotees perform shocking rituals of self-mutilation, so it's not for the squeamish.

NEED TO KNOW
MAP K3

Sunday Walking Street Market: **MAP P5**; Thalang Road (between Phuket and Yaowarat roads); open 4–10pm Sun

Phuket Cultural Centre: **MAP K2**; 21 Thepkasatri Road; 07621 1959 (ext 148); open 8:30am–4:30pm Mon–Fri; closed weekends and public hols

Naka Weekend Market: **MAP J3**; open 4–10pm Sat & Sun

■ Avoid walking tours at midday – the streets can be unbearably warm.

■ Try the iced coffee at Tunk-Ka Cafe atop Rang Hill.

■ Sample a chili dog from the Tuk-Tuk Diner, which parks at the west end of the Thalang Road market.

Historic Buildings in Phuket Town

Blue Elephant Restaurant, set in elegant grounds

① Blue Elephant Restaurant

MAP N5 ▪ 96 Krabi Road ▪ 07635 4355 ▪ Open 11am–9pm daily

Next door to the Chinpracha House, this former governor's mansion is a fine-dining venue and cookery school.

② Standard Chartered Bank

MAP P5 ▪ Phang-Nga Road ▪ Open 9am–4:30pm Tue–Sun

This graceful Sino-Portuguese building once housed the country's oldest foreign bank. Inside, there is a small public museum dedicated to Phuket's Baba (Peranakan) culture.

③ Thai Hua Museum

MAP P5 ▪ 28 Krabi Road ▪ 07621 1224 ▪ Open 9am–5pm daily ▪ Closed public holidays ▪ Adm

This distinctive building was once used as a schoolhouse. The museum provides an excellent overview of Phuket's tin-mining era. Displays cover the daily life of the Chinese immigrants, architecture, and archival photographs of old Phuket.

④ Chinpracha House

MAP N5 ▪ 98 Krabi Road ▪ 07621 1281 ▪ Open 9am–4:30pm daily ▪ Adm

This 19th-century mansion has served as a backdrop for several Hollywood films including Oliver Stone's 1993 movie *Heaven and Earth*, based on the Vietnam War. Now a museum of domestic life, the house stands as a timeless reminder of an earlier era.

⑤ Rush Coffee

MAP K3 ▪ Soi Romanee (Romani) ▪ 06207 5239 ▪ Open 8am–5pm daily

Located on a charming street lined with wonderful buildings, this classic two-story Sino-Portuguese shop house features nice period decor. A great place for people-watching, the café brews some of the best coffee in town.

⑥ Dibuk Restaurant

MAP P5 ▪ 69 Dibuk Road ▪ 07621 4138 ▪ Open 11am–11pm Mon–Sat

Another fine example of century-old architecture, this building now serves as a relaxing restaurant known for its delicious Thai and French cuisine *(see p86)*. The old Chinese-style house features soft interior lighting and antique fans.

Facade of the Thai Hua Museum

⑦ Phuket Philatelic Museum

MAP P5 ▪ Montri Road ▪ 07621 6951
▪ Open 9am–5pm Tue–Sat

Also known as the Post Office Museum, this 20th-century building (see p47) has displays detailing the history of the Thai postal service.

⑧ Phuket Provincial Hall

MAP Q4 ▪ Narisorn Road
▪ 07621 1366 ▪ Open 9am–5pm daily

The Provincial Hall was built in the early 1910s. It originally featured 99 doors and no windows, and is said to be the first reinforced concrete building in Thailand.

⑨ The Memory At On On Hotel

MAP P5 ▪ 19 Phang-Nga Road
▪ 07636 3700

This Sino-Portuguese building (see p117) is Phuket's first hotel. You may recognize it from British director Danny Boyle's movie The Beach (2000).

⑩ China Inn Café and Restaurant

MAP P5 ▪ 20 Thalang Road ▪ 07635 6239 ▪ Open 11am–5pm Mon–Sat

Wooden doors, Chinese lanterns, and tiled floors decorate the entrance of this restaurant-meets-antique store, set in a classic Sino-Portuguese-style house. The store, which has a wonderful collection of old Chinese artifacts, occupies the interior and the restaurant is set in the backyard.

Entrance to the China Inn Café

ARCHITECTURAL LEGACY

During the tin boom of the late 19th and early 20th centuries, countless Chinese immigrants arrived on Phuket seeking to capitalize on the island's new-found economic opportunities. The most successful tin barons built mansions in the Sino-Portuguese architectural style, which was derived from early European settlements. Examples abound in Phuket Town, particularly the shop houses and mansions on Dibuk, Thalang, Phang Nga, Rassada, Yaowarat, and Phuket roads.

TOP 10
CHARACTERISTICS OF SINO-PORTUGUESE ARCHITECTURAL STYLE

1 Romanesque arched colonnades (porticoes)

2 Inner courtyards (airwells)

3 Exterior windows with Romanesque arches and shutters

4 Double doors and double shutters

5 Terracotta tiled roofs

6 Tiled floors in ornate patterns

7 Victorian ornamentation

8 Chinese signage

9 Ornamental wrought-iron gates

10 Eaves decorated with ceramic shards

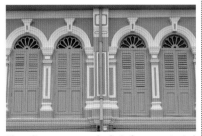
These Romanesque arched windows are a typical element of the Sino-Portuguese architectural style.

TOP 10 ★ Wat Chalong

Historical records are unclear, but Wat Chalong was probably first built during the reign of King Rama II (r.1809–24). However, the temple has undergone many renovations since it was first erected. The complex features sacred imagery, including sculptures and murals of the Buddha's life. The holiest object is a bone fragment of the Buddha, now set in the Grand Pagoda. The temple is called Wat Chaitararam by royal decree, but everyone knows it as Wat Chalong.

1 Architecture
The temple's colorful, multitiered sloping roofs **(above)**, ornate exterior, and interior decorations are very picturesque. The Grand Pagoda's towering spire and glittering window frames are among its other visual highlights.

2 Fortune Telling
Fortune tellers sit inside the temple's main hall. They shake two cans of numbered bamboo sticks until one falls out. The number corresponds to a paper slip inside a wooden cabinet. Take it and ask for a translation.

3 Merit-Making
Thai Buddhists visit temples and pay respect to the Buddha and other spiritual leaders to accumulate merit, in the belief that such deeds will benefit one's position in this life and future lives **(left)**.

4 Temple History
During an uprising of Chinese tin workers in the late 19th century, many local Thais fled to Wat Chalong for protection. The temple's then abbot, Luang Pho Chaem, provided shelter to the people and was later honored for this by King Rama V (r.1868–1910).

5 Firecrackers
Devotees burst firecrackers in thanks for answered prayers. The fireworks pop inside a beehive-shaped structure located outside, near the sermon hall.

6 Buddha Image

Known as Poh Than Jao Wat, the main Buddha image (left) is within Wat Chalong's western hall. It is flanked by two statues, one of which supposedly depicts a local man who won several lotteries after praying to the image.

7 Wax Figures

Lifelike models of former temple abbots can be found inside a special exhibition space. Visitors pay tribute to these spiritual leaders to make merit.

WAT CHALONG FAIR

First held in 1954, the annual Wat Chalong Fair transforms the temple grounds into a bustling entertainment venue featuring live music performances, sermons, and an endless variety of delicious local cuisine. Vendors also set up carnival games, ferris wheels, and merry-go-rounds. The eight-day festival coincides with the Chinese New Year and it historically marked the end of a local farm harvest.

NEED TO KNOW

MAP J4 ▪ Chao Fah Nok Road; 07621 1036, 07638 1893

Open 7am–5pm daily

▪ Dress conservatively and remove your shoes before entering certain buildings. Don't turn your back on or point your feet at an image of the Buddha.

▪ Street food vendors, selling everything from fried grasshoppers to grilled chicken and pork skewers marinated in chilli sauce, congregate outside the temple.

8 Wall Paintings

Inside the Grand Pagoda, wall paintings show events from the life of Siddhartha Gautama, who became the Buddha after gaining enlightenment. Notable depictions include him teaching his disciples and receiving offerings (above).

9 Gilded Statues

Cast in bronze, these depictions of former temple abbots are covered in flecks of gold foil. Visitors offer donations and make merit by affixing small pieces of gold-colored foil onto the statues.

10 Grand Pagoda

This 197-ft (60-m) tall golden pagoda enshrines a bone splinter of the Buddha. Brought from Sri Lanka in 1999, it is housed inside a *chedi* (stupa) on the third story of the pagoda (below).

TOP 10 ⭐ Patong

Travelers dreaming of a sleepy tropical hideaway might want to look elsewhere – Patong is full of action. The most popular tourist area in Phuket, it features a great range of hotels, from luxury resorts to budget stays, restaurants, and nightlife. Add seemingly endless shopping options, wild entertainment venues, and a range of daytime activities and it's no wonder that Patong has earned a name for itself as Phuket's ultimate high-energy playground.

1 Patong Beach
Patong (above), Phuket's most popular tourist beach, offers a range of attractions. It also has more laid-back areas – for peace and quiet, the northern end of the beach is best.

2 Massage and Spa Treatments
Thailand is known for its world-class hospitality, exemplified by its traditional massage treatments (left) and spas, which are ubiquitous in Patong.

3 Muay Thai Fights
Don't miss a chance to see this Thai martial art. Five three-minute rounds, accompanied by romping music, are preceded by the pomp and ceremony of ancient pre-fight rituals.

NEED TO KNOW

MAP H3

Patong Boxing Stadium (Muay Thai fights): **MAP P1**; 2/59 Sai Nam Yen Road; 07634 5578; adm B1,300 upward; www.boxingstadiumpatong.com

Illuzion Nightclub: 31 Bangla Road; 07668 3030

Bangla Boxing Stadium (Muay Thai fights): **MAP P2**; Bangla Road; 06406 15050; adm B1,300 upward

Simon Cabaret: **MAP N3**; Sirirach Road, Patong Beach; 08788 86888; adm; open 7:30–9:30pm daily; www.phuket-simon cabaret.com

Tiger Nightclub: 49 Bangla Road; 06549 49099

Seduction Nightclub: 39/1 Bangla Road; 07634 0215; www.seductiondisco.com

■ Be sure to bargain with vendors at the market.

■ Street carts serve some of the best Thai food.

6 Watersports

If you enjoy getting an adrenaline fix right at the beach, Patong is the place for you. From wave running and speed-boat rides to parasailing **(left)** and banana boats, Patong Bay offers a range of exhilarating marine activities.

A MATTER OF PERSPECTIVE

Some foreign travelers are shocked by Patong's extremely liberal sexual norms, parti-cularly after the sun goes down. The Bangla Road area comes to life after sunset, but it's risqué nightlife does not make it suitable for families with young children. However, Bangla Road is not all Patong has to offer and it is easy to avoid if not to one's liking.

8 Street Markets

The night market sells everything from T-shirts to Buddha images, and prices are low. Those near the beach road offer the widest choice.

4 Fresh Seafood

At sundown, restaurants along the beachfront promenade display the day's fresh catch packed on ice. Snapper, grouper, shrimp, crabs, lobster, and other delicious seafood can be individually selected, grilled, and seasoned to your taste.

9 Bangla Road

The central vein of Patong is ablaze at night with neon lights **(below)** and has music blaring from every direction.

5 Nightclubs

If you're looking for a place to party, Patong's nightlife is infamously rowdy. Popular spots include Kudo Beach Club, the Bay Hill Resort, Illuzion Nightclub, Seduction Nightclub, and Tiger Nightclub.

7 Cabaret Shows

These shows, star-ring performers from the LGBTQ+ community, have been thrilling audiences for decades. The most popular venue, Simon Cabaret **(left)**, puts on two shows in an extrava-gantly decorated theater.

10 Restaurants

Patong's culinary scene is seriously under-rated. Whether you're looking for a classic Pad Thai or Georgian dump-lings, you'll find it in the town's many restaurants. Seek out Il Pomodoro, Tusk or Georgia.

TOP 10 ⭐ Khao Phra Thaeo Royal Forest and Wildlife Reserve

Spread over 9 sq miles (23 sq km) of virgin rain forest, this national park in northeast Phuket provides one of the last remaining natural habitats for endemic and endangered animal species on the island. Visitors can immerse themselves in the jungles that once covered much of the island as Khao Phra Thaeo offers pristine forest, raw hiking trails, and picturesque waterfalls. There is also a rehabilitation center where gibbons receive care and treatment, as well as plenty of rare plants, flowers, and trees.

Gibbon Rehabilitation Project ①

The calls of gibbons ring through the forest around the center, which was established in 1992 to care for animals that had previously been living in captivity. It reintroduces some gibbons **(right)** into the wild.

Wildlife Conservation Development and Extension Centre ②

Located near the base of Ton Sai Waterfall, this visitor center offers lectures on the park's history and purpose, as well as trail guides, brochures, and limited, basic accommodations.

Bang Pae Waterfall ③

The larger of the park's two major waterfalls, Bang Pae **(left)** plummets down and forms a pool ideal for a cool, refreshing dip. The easy walk from the parking lot to the waterfall takes around ten minutes.

Ton Sai Waterfall ④

A scenic little waterfall in the center of the wildlife sanctuary, this is an enjoyable place to spend an afternoon. Climb the rocky paths near the falls, but be careful, since the rocks can get slippery.

NEED TO KNOW

MAP D5

Visitor Center: 254 Moo 2, Thepkasattri Road, Thalang; 07631 1998; open 8:30am–4:30pm daily; adm B200 (kids B100)

Zipline Tour: Cable Jungle Adventure Phuket; 232/17 Bansuaneramit, Moo 8; 081977 4904; open 9am–5pm daily; adm B2,150; www.cablejunglephuket.com

Gibbon Rehabilitation Project: Pa Khlock, Thalang; 08859 09714; open 9am–4:30pm daily; www.gibbonproject.org

Wildlife Conservation Development and Extension Centre: Highway 4027; 07621 1067; open 9am–4pm daily

■ Heavy rain is common, especially during summer.

■ Try the Bang Rong Floating Restaurant near Bang Pae Waterfall.

8 Trekking
A scenic 5-mile- (8-km-) long jungle path links Ton Sai and Bang Pae waterfalls. At the visitor center near Ton Sai, trekkers can hire an experienced guide, who will be able to point out some of the park's animal and plant species.

9 Virgin Rain Forest
Evergreen trees, bamboo forests, orchids, ferns, and mosses can all be found in Khao Phra Thaeo, the last tract of virgin rain forest on the island. The area that surrounds the sanctuary includes several large rubber tree plantations.

10 Wildlife
The sanctuary's natural environment is home to a vast number of species, including wild boar, macaque monkeys, gibbons, langurs, and various types of deer.

5 Zipline Tour
Sail with the birds and monkeys through the jungle canopy. Set just outside the forest reserve, the course is over a mile (2 km) long. Experienced guides take you through a full safety demonstration. It's a bit of a hike to the start of the course (above).

6 Flora
An endangered plant known as the white-backed palm is one of the highlights of the Khao Phra Thaeo Royal Forest and Wildlife Reserve. First documented by a German botanist in the 1950s, this elegant fan-shaped palm is unique to southern Thailand.

7 Bird-Watching
Northern Phuket is a true paradise for bird-watchers. Inside the sanctuary, you can spot flowerpeckers (left), bulbuls, sunbirds, green Leafbirds, red-billed Malkohas, Asian fairy-bluebirds, blue-winged Pitta, and Brahminy Kites.

CAPTIVE GIBBONS

In many Thai tourist areas, local touts carry baby gibbons around to lure foreigners into taking photographs with the cute little primates. In exchange, the touts ask for a little money. If approached, keep in mind that the gibbons are being kept illegally, and that many of them lose their lives when hunters try to capture them for the tourist trade. The small Gibbon Rehabilitation Project at the Khao Phra Thaeo Royal Forest and Wildlife Reserve works to protect these animals.

🔟 ⭐ Sirinat National Park

A rugged, pristine pine-lined strip runs along Phuket's northwest coast and marks three largely undeveloped beaches: Mai Khao, Nai Yang, and Nai Thon. Although this land forms the Sirinat National Park, over three quarters of the reserve's 35 sq miles (90 sq km) is marine territory. The clean waters feature large, healthy coral reefs, and Mai Khao Beach has become a well-known sea turtle nesting site. At the northern end of Sirinat is an unspoiled mangrove forest.

① Upmarket Resorts

The beaches of northern Phuket are home to upscale resorts (see p112) that blend well with the national park surroundings. The JW Marriott (below), Sala Phuket, and Anantara, among others, offer 5-star luxury.

② Camping on Nai Yang Beach

Visitors can bring their own tent to this beautiful beach, or rent one, priced at B225 per night, from the national park's Visitor Center. Different types of bedding and sleeping mats are also available. The well-kept campgrounds offer guests toilet and shower facilities.

③ Visitor Center

At the southern end of Mai Khao Beach, the Visitor Center offers maps and rents out tents, including budget bungalows, at the north end of Nai Yang Beach.

NEED TO KNOW

Visitor Center: MAP B3; 89/1 Moo 1, Tambon Nai Yang; 07632 7152; open 8:30am–4:30pm daily; www.park.dnp.go.th

Mai Khao Marine Turtle Foundation: MAP B1; 231 Moo3, Mai Khao, Talang, Phuket; 07633 8040; open 9:30am–3:30pm daily; www.maikhaomarine turtlefoundation.org

Scuba Diving and Snorkeling: **MAP B4;** Paradise Diving; 116 Moo 5, Sakoo Village, Thalang; 07632 8278; adm (B3,300); www.paradise-diving.com

■ Those who cannot afford luxury resorts can pitch a tent on the beach.

■ Excellent fresh fish is served by the string of local seafood restaurants set along Route 402.

Sirinat National Park

9 Nai Thon Beach

This quiet beach **(left)** north of Bang Tao retains its sleepy and natural feel despite the coming of better road access. Small coral reefs located off either tip of the beach provide great opportunities for snorkeling.

5 Mangroves

A mangrove forest **(left)** can be found at the northern end of Mai Khao Beach. These unique trees, with their tangled roots visible above the shoreline, are crucial in maintaining the ecological balance.

6 Scuba Diving

Off the coast of northern Phuket lies an interesting scuba diving site – an old tin dredger that sank off the coast of Ko Waew. Reachable by boat from Nai Thon Beach, the 164-ft- (50-m-) long wreck rests at a depth of 53 ft (16 m).

7 Snorkeling

There are many opportunities for snorkeling near the rocky headlands of Nai Yang Beach. Masks, fins, and snorkels can be hired. Look out for colorful schools of fish.

8 Mai Khao Beach

Phuket's longest beach **(below)** is a thin, undulating strip that slopes steeply down into the sea. Lined with magnificent screw pines, and with very little intrusive development, it remains one of the island's natural wonders.

TURTLE CONSERVATION

The Mai Khao Marine Turtle Foundation, along with several Mai Khao Beach resorts, releases dozens of green turtles into the Andaman Sea each year to raise funds for the endangered sea turtles. The conservation effort also includes beach- and reef-cleaning projects. The number of turtles returning to Mai Khao Beach has dwindled, but it is hoped that the annual nesting site will be preserved.

10 Nature Trail

At the northern end of Mai Khao Beach, an elevated walkway loops through the mangrove forest, with signs pointing out native plant species, including black myrsina, Lady's Nails quisqualis, red cycas, and mountain ebony.

4 Sea Turtles

Giant sea turtles **(above)** return to Mai Khao Beach every year between November and March to lay their eggs. If you spot a turtle on the beach, do not disturb it or touch its eggs.

Following pages Floating bamboo-raft houses on Cheow Laan Lake, Khao Sok National Park

TOP 10 ⭐ Nai Harn Beach

Framing an idyllic bay on the island's southwestern tip, Nai Harn Beach remains one of Phuket's most pristine waterfronts. The half-mile- (1-km-) long, white-sand beach is flanked by green hills and lapped by turquoise waters. While nearby Nai Harn village has been modernized with cafés, art shops, and guesthouses, the beach and surrounding hills still maintain a tranquil, non-commercial vibe, with hotels congregated along only one end. During the high season, a number of private yachts drop anchor in the bay, making Nai Harn their temporary home.

4 Nai Harn Buddhist Monastery

Behind Nai Harn Beach, this spiritual center **(below)**, which owns the beachfront, is said to be partly responsible for keeping it unspoiled. Visit at dawn, when locals make merit by offering food to the monks.

1 Nai Harn Beach

Relax under a sun umbrella, catch a tan on the powdery white sand, or wade out into the emerald waters – Nai Harn Beach **(above)** will satisfy even the toughest critic's ideal of a tropical paradise.

3 Surfing

The gentle waves and sandy shoreline here attract many boogie-boarders; surfers go for the sandy beach break at the southern end or the reef break to the north. Beware of the undertow.

2 Yanui Beach

Just south of Nai Harn Beach, and accessible via the road that leads to Phromthep Cape, this small V-shaped stretch of sand **(below)** offers seclusion amid the shade of coconut palms. It also has a small restaurant and some great spots for snorkeling.

5 Ao Sane Beach

With its rocky shoreline and rough slope down into the sea, Ao Sane Beach **(above)** does not see hordes of swimmers. However, it is a prime spot for snorkelers, who claim that the visibility and nearby corals are among the best in Nai Harn.

6 Nai Harn Lake

Bicyclists and joggers enjoy the paved half-mile (1-km) route encircling this inland freshwater lake. With sea breezes, it is also a pleasant picnic destination. Popular cafés and bars can be found on the lake's north-western shore.

7 Muay Thai

A number of Muay Thai gyms have been established in Nai Harn Village. Visitors can punch some heavy bags, skip rope, and hit the pads with former professional Thai fighters.

8 Phromthep Cape

Crowds flock to the beach each evening to witness the vivid sunset over the Andaman Sea at sundown. Phromthep Cape **(right)** also has a market, restaurant, elephant shrine, and lighthouse.

9 Beachside Lunch

Shaded by a canopy of umbrellas and pine trees, the open-air restaurants at Nai Harn Beach serve reasonably priced fresh fruit shakes, sandwiches, and a wide selection of Thai dishes.

10 Windmill Viewpoint

Perched high on the hills overlooking Nai Harn Beach, the Phromthep Alternative Energy Station offers stunning views. Paragliders also launch from here to land on the beach.

EXPLOSIVE GROWTH

Until the 21st century, the quiet beach and village at Nai Harn were still unknown. The sleepy village had a few open-air restaurants and guesthouses, but not much more. Since 2010, like the rest of Phuket, development began, and residences, resorts, and restaurants started popping up throughout the town. Today, the beach is still one of Phuket's most beautiful, but attracts a lot more visitors than it did in the past.

NEED TO KNOW

MAP H6

Sinbi Muay Thai: **MAP H5**; 100/15 Moo 7, Sai Yuan Road, Rawai; 093 690 3322; www.sinbi-muaythai.com

Kingka Muay Thai: **MAP H5**; 43/42, Sai Yuan Road, Rawai; 093 576 9104; www.kingkamuaythai.com

- It is a long way from Nai Harn village to the beach. Rent a car or motorbike to travel back and forth.

- Drink fresh coconut water while at the beach.

★ Kata Beach

Located just south of Karon, the scenic Kata Beach, comprising two bays separated by a small rocky headland, offers an ideal balance of tropical scenery and well-developed tourism infrastructure. Kata has a number of high-end resorts, making it a popular destination for couples and families. Palm trees fringe the white-sand beach, and the clear turquoise waters offer good swimming conditions throughout the year. Visitors can even swim to nearby Ko Pu, a small island, passing beautiful coral reefs along the way.

1 Nightlife
Less wild than Patong, Kata still offers plenty for night owls. Most bars **(above)** are open-air, dotted with festive lights, and play music aimed to please a crowd that wants to relax and chat.

2 Shopping
The beach vendors in Kata sell beachwear, coconuts, and snacks, while the off-beach stalls offer a wide range of inexpensive clothing and souvenirs.

3 Spa and Massage Treatments
Traditional Thai massages are available at numerous venues, including the canopy-covered massage beds along the beach.

4 Thai Cooking Classes
Learn how to make Thai curries and much more **(below)** at one of the many cookery classes in Kata. One is hosted by the upscale Boathouse Restaurant, or there's the Kata Thai Cooking Class.

NEED TO KNOW

MAP H5

The Boathouse Restaurant: Kata Beach; 07633 0015–7; adm (for cooking class) B2,200; www.boathouse-phuket.com

Kata Thai Cooking Class: 5 Ket Kwan Road, Kata Beach; 09195 45563; www.katathaicooking.com

Kata Temple: MAP H4; Patak Road, Karon; open daily

A Blanket & A Pillow: **MAP H4;** 0/1 Laemsai Road Tumbon, Karon; open 10:30am–7:30pm Tue–Sun

■ Karon Viewpoint is a wonderful place to watch the sunset.

■ Wine lovers can visit The Boathouse Restaurant, whose excellent wine list features more than 800 labels.

7 Watersports

The best season for surfing (left) in Kata is from May to October. The waters around Kata are great for beginners since the waves are not too large. The southern end is best for surfing, but if that's not for you, rent a kayak from the north end of the beach.

DEVELOPMENT

During the 1970s, Kata was known as a low-budget backpacker's destination offering inexpensive beach bungalows and cheap guesthouses. However, when Club Med opened its doors in 1985, the area started turning upscale. Today, Kata mostly caters to well-to-do family travelers. Low-cost rooms can still be found along the inland roads, while most of the beachfront properties have been snapped up by high-end developers.

9 Restaurants

Kata has a variety of restaurants, from swanky ones, such as The Boathouse Restaurant to laidback options. Visit the beach café A Blanket & A Pillow, which is known for its sundowner parties.

5 Karon Viewpoint

On the coastal road south toward Nai Harn, this viewpoint (above) provides gorgeous views of the island. Look north and you'll see three white-sand beaches along the coastline.

8 Kata Noi

The more secluded of Kata's beaches, Kata Noi (below), located just south of Kata Yai, generally offers more space and privacy than its larger counterpart, especially during the low season.

10 Kata Yai

When people talk about Kata, they are usually referring to Kata Yai, which is the larger of the two Kata bays, and offers more resorts and activities. The beach is separated from Kata Noi, which is much quieter, by a small rocky headland.

6 Kata Temple

This Buddhist wat lies at the base of the mountains behind Kata town. Formally known as Wat Kittisangkaram, it dates from the 1800s, but it was rebuilt. It is rarely visited by tourists due to its modern buildings.

TOP 10 ⭐ Similan Islands National Park

Soft white-sand beaches and emerald-colored waters are the foundations of this island paradise. Renowned as one of the world's top scuba diving destinations, the underwater world here is stunningly beautiful, with magnificent corals, colorful fish, and dramatic rock formations. The nine Similan islands also offer remarkable snorkeling. Plan your trip with a tour operator based on the mainland – diving equipment is not available on the islands.

1 Anita's Reef
This colorful reef (**below**) spreads across two Similan Islands, and is punctuated by large, dramatic boulders. Offering a relatively easy dive, Anita's Reef is often one of the first stops for live-aboard trips.

2 Ko Similan
Home to Donald Duck Bay (**above**), named for the rock formation that resembles the cartoon character, Ko Similan is a perfect spot for you to pitch your tent. The island also has scenic walking trails, so carry sturdy shoes and a camera.

3 Live-Aboard Boats
One of the best ways to experience the dive sites around the Similans is to join a multiday trip on a live-aboard boat (**below**) offering guests several dives each day.

4 Christmas Point
Deep shelves, which are populated by white-tip reef sharks as well as ribbon eels, make this site very popular with divers and under-water photographers.

NEED TO KNOW

Visitor Center: **MAP D2**; 93 Moo 5, Tambon Lam Kaen; 07645 3272; open 9am–5pm daily; adm B500 (kids B300; plus B200 per person for drivers); www.park.dnp.go.th

■ The park is closed May through October.

■ Food options are limited, so pack enough food if you have special dietary needs.

5 Beacon Reef

The longest reef in the Similan Islands, Beacon Reef also marks the place where the *Atlantis X* sank, with no casualties, in 2002. Today, the sunken vessel, now resting on a sloping coral wall, is one of the reef's most popular underwater attractions and provides home to a wide variety of marine life.

Ko Bangu

53 miles (85 km)   15 miles (25 km)

Ko Similan

Ko Payu

Ko Miang   Ko Ha

Similan Islands National Park

9 Richelieu Rock

Well known for its abundant marine life, Richelieu Rock has been renowned as a diving site since whale sharks and manta rays were spotted here.

DIVING PRECAUTIONS

Scuba diving is very safe when done correctly, but it can be dangerous – even deadly – for the untrained diver. Reliable dive companies require all participants to have a PADI (Professional Association of Diving Instructors) certification. A number of companies on Phuket are licensed to provide courses and certification. The PADI course for beginners is called "Open Water Diver" and can be completed in a few days. Visit www.padi.com for a list of PADI dive centers in Thailand.

7 Ko Bon

Located in a protected bay and featuring one of Thailand's only vertical dive walls, this site, off Ko Bon, provides marvelous opportunities to see leopard sharks **(left)** and manta rays.

10 East of Eden

A brilliantly colorful reef, East of Eden is one of the most popular dive sites in the Similan Islands. Teeming with fish, it offers a wide diversity of marine life – coral, sea fans, and more.

6 Elephant Head Rock

The largest pinnacle in the Similan Islands juts above the water in a peculiar shape that lends this dive site its name. With its underwater caverns, tunnels, and swim-throughs, this site is home to numerous fish, including small, black-tip reef sharks.

8 Ko Miang

Home to the national park headquarters, Ko Miang **(right)** is the second biggest island in the Similans. Visitors will find campsites and basic bungalows (some with air-conditioned rooms). A large tent can be rented here for around B450 a night.

Khao Sok National Park

With a landmass of more than 270 sq miles (700 sq km), this park, about 110 miles (177 km) north of Phuket, is southern Thailand's largest virgin forest. Older and more diverse than even the Amazon rain forest, Khao Sok is home to numerous animal and plant species, and has breathtaking natural scenery. Nature lovers will find inspiration in the park's majestic limestone cliffs, its rough jungle trails, and its beautiful, placid waterways.

1 Canoeing and Kayaking

The scenic Sok river offers a relaxing way to experience the park's natural wonders. Kayak or canoe through lush jungle, past towering limestone rocks. You may spot snakes, hornbills, and long-tail macaque monkeys.

3 Cheow Laan Lake

Surrounded by verdant forests and towering mountains, this beautiful lake (above) was formed when Ratchaprapha Dam was constructed in 1982. It makes for a perfect retreat for those looking for a quiet day.

4 Raft Houses

Thatched-roof floating raft houses (below) line the banks of Cheow Laan Lake, and visitors may stay in them for a night or longer. When the sun rises in the morning, dive into the lake for a brisk morning swim or enjoy a canoe ride.

2 Waterfalls

There are several scenic waterfalls (above) in the park, although finding them sometimes requires the assistance of a local guide. Bang Hua Raet, Wang Yao, and Wing Hin waterfalls are all located within a 1-mile (2-km) radius of the park headquarters.

6 Wildlife

A bird-watcher's paradise, Khao Sok National Park has numerous bird and mammal species *(see pp34–5)* including hornbills, kingfishers **(left)**, wild pigs, eagles, and much more. Wildlife enthusiasts may even spot Asiatic black bears.

BUA PHUT

These huge red flowers, whose diameter can reach up to 35 inches (90 cm), are popular with visitors, although finding one in bloom often requires good timing and the help of a local guide. Known scientifically as *Rafflesia kerrii*, the flowers are abundant from January to March, and have a pungent odor to attract flies for pollination. The species is endangered.

7 Night Safaris

As some animal species, such as the loris and the leopard cat, can only be spotted after dark, night river safaris are a popular way to see these unique creatures. Canoes or bamboo rafts are used to quietly glide down the Sok river.

8 Bamboo Rafting

Float down the Sok on a unique watercraft fashioned out of lengths of bamboo, taking in the trees, magnificent mountains, and wildlife. You'll stop for lunch in a riverside restaurant.

10 Caves

Experience the tantalizing darkness of some of the park's many caves, including the popular Tham Nam Talu and Ha Roi Rai. These grottoes have fascinating stalagmites and stalactites **(below)**, as well as legions of bats.

9 Jungle Trekking

Walk along the well-beaten paths with a guide through the untamed, lush jungle. The scope for trekking is exceptional, with caves, waterfalls, and lakes.

❷ ❾   ❹ ❸

Cheow Laan Lake

ℹ Park HQ

401

Sok

401

❶❽ ❺

Khao Sok National Park

5 Romanee Hot Spring

Located just south of the National Park, this natural hot spring has been attractively developed with tiled pools, and the mineral waters are excellent for relieving muscle stress from strenuous trekking activities.

NEED TO KNOW

Visitor Center: **MAP F1**; Moo 6, Khlong Sok; 07739 5139; open 8am–4pm daily; adm B300 (kids B150); www.park.dnp.go.th

Raft Houses, Bamboo Rafting, Jungle Trekking: **MAP F1**; Elephant Hills Tented Camp; 170 Moo 7, Tambon Khlong Sok; 05200 1186; www. elephanthills.com

Canoeing and Kayaking, Adventure Trips: **MAP F1**; Paddle Asia; 18/58 Radanusorn; 08189 36558; www.paddleasia.com

▪ Khao Sok can be visited on a day trip from Phuket, but it is better appreciated with more time.

▪ Romanee Hot Spring visits are organized via Hotel Khao Sok *(www. hotelkhaosok.com/tours)*.

Animal Species in Khao Sok National Park

Malaysian tapir on the move

1 Malaysian Tapir

With its distinctive proboscis, this large-bodied herbivore looks somewhat like a pig with an elephant's trunk. The tapir's black color provides camouflage, so that, when it is lying down, the animal looks like a rock.

2 Bamboo Rat

Sporting short bulky bodies covered in spiky fur, these nocturnal rodents live predominantly in bamboo thickets, as well as in grasslands and forests. Bamboo rats have sharp teeth and claws that are ideally suited to digging the burrows in which they sleep during the day.

3 Barking Deer

Also known as muntjac, these small, brown-haired deer have short antlers. Commonly seen in the park, they are called barking deer because they are known to bark when they sense danger.

Barking deer

4 Tiger

Many of Thailand's 200 to 250 remaining wild tigers are believed to be living in Khao Sok, although you are unlikely to catch a glimpse of one. If you are lucky, however, you might come across tiger tracks.

5 Cobras

Khao Sok is home to four different species of cobra – the monocled, spitting, king, and Asian cobras. The king cobra is the world's longest venomous snake, reaching lengths greater than 16 ft (5 m).

Striking hornbill, perched in a tree

6 Hornbill

The hornbill's distinctive yellow/red horn and long down-curved mandible make the bird easily identifiable. Feeding on fruits, berries, insects, small mammals, and eggs, hornbills often reside in dense forests. Many species can be spotted in Khao Sok National Park.

7 Tarantula

These massive spiders tend to dwell inside underground burrows. The ones found in Thailand move fast and are known to be aggressive, so give the tarantula plenty of space if you encounter one in the wild.

8 Clouded Leopard
Exceptional climbers, with large feet and powerful claws, clouded leopards have a beautiful yellow-brown coat with distinctive cloud markings. The animal sleeps in trees and can hang upside down from branches by its hind paws. Its prey includes small mammals and birds, among other creatures.

9 Elephant
Wild elephants still roam Khao Sok National Park but sadly, these majestic creatures, the symbol of Thailand, are an endangered species. Herds of elephants can occasionally be spotted in forested areas near watering holes and elsewhere.

10 Malaysian Sun Bear
A small bear that generally weighs less than 143 lb (65 kgs), this threatened animal resides in dense forests, where it sleeps and suns itself in trees. An omnivore, the sun bear has no real predators, other than the occasional human.

Malaysian Sun Bear foraging

HISTORY OF THE PARK

Before it was declared a national park in 1980, the forest-covered land known as Khao Sok was a wilderness that stretched to Myanmar. Few roads bisected this territory, and animal populations, including tigers, flourished. When Ratchaprapha Dam was built in the mid-1980s, numerous trees were chopped down. Poachers also threatened the stability of some animal populations. Today, under the protection of the National Park Service, Khao Sok is home to lots of species, and many poachers have become conservationists.

Liana vines string themselves from tree to tree, forming sky bridges used by wildlife to get about.

TOP 10
FLORA IN KHAO SOK NATIONAL PARK

1 Rain forest vegetation
2 Coconut palms
3 Buttressed roots trees
4 Ficus trees
5 Bamboo trees
6 Tropical pitcher plants
7 Dipterocarps trees
8 *Rafflesia kerrii*
9 Banana trees
10 Liana vines

🔟 ⭐ Phang Nga Bay

Just east of Phuket over 40 small islands dot the brilliantly azure waters of Phang Nga Bay. Wind and water have eroded these limestone karst islets into a variety of extraordinary shapes that tower above the water's surface. This National Park is home to an abundance of flora and fauna that thrive amid the crevices, arches, tide pools, caves, and coastal forests. Paddling a sea kayak among the grandeur of these soaring peaks is an experience to savor, but motorized boats can also transport you around the bay.

James Bond Island ③

The backdrop for 007's infamous duel in *The Man with the Golden Gun*, the island **(right)**– also known as Ko Khao Phing Kan – today represents one of Phuket's most popular island day trips.

④ Sea Caves

These unique geological formations are magnificent, however, you can only pass them during low tides. There are caves on the mainland and the islands.

① Kayaking and Canoeing

Paddle through extraordinary aquatic grottoes that open into magnificent open-air lagoons **(above)**, populated by colorful birds such as hornbills and kingfishers. The pristine jungle scenery beside these lagoons is also worth exploring on foot.

⑤ Ko Phanak

This island is favored by sea kayakers because of its abundance of hongs – amazing hidden sea chambers that are open to the sky but enclosed by the island, and accessible only through caves.

⑥ Khao Khian

Also known as "Writing Hill," this cave has ancient drawings of humans, birds, fish, and other marine life, dating back some 3,000 years.

Ko Panyee ②

Most of Ko Panyee's landmass is consumed by a towering limestone rock. Due to this geology, it is difficult to build on the island, and the village **(right)** has been constructed on stilts above the shallow waters of the south coast.

7 Traditional Junk Boat Cruises

One of Phuket's classic boat cruises, the traditional junk-rigged schooner *June Bahtra* explores the islands and limestone cliffs of Phang Nga Bay, while a separate evening cruise trip provides sundown dinner and cocktails.

9 National Park Headquarters

The park headquarters, near Phang Nga town, features a raised walkway through a mangrove wetland, as well as boat rentals, a restaurant, and good bungalows. Phang Nga town pier is also a staging point for boats to the islands.

Phang Nga Bay

10 Mangrove Wetlands

Phang Nga Bay has the largest mangrove forests in Thailand, with the best on the mainland at the north end of the bay. Kayaks let you get up close to their twisted underwater root systems **(left)**.

8 Ko Yao Noi

With unspoiled coastlines, pristine beaches, and pretty thatched-roof bungalows, this island – part of a two-island group – exudes tranquil vibes.

NEED TO KNOW

Visitor Center: **MAP F2**; 80 Moo 1, Tambon Ban Tha Dan, Ko Panyee; 07648 1188; open 8am–4pm daily; adm B300 (kids B100); www.park.dnp.go.th

Kayaking and Canoeing: **MAP F2** ; Paddle Asia; 18/ 58 Radanusorn; 08189 365 58; www.paddleasia.com

Traditional Junk Boat Cruises: **MAP F2**; Asian Oasis; open 8am–6pm & 4–9pm daily; adm B35,000 onward; www.asian-oasis.com

Sea Cave Tours: **MAP F2**; John Gray's Sea Canoe; adm B32,000 onward; www.johngray-seacanoe.com

■ Hire a long-tail boat at Nai Harn Beach to visit some of the islands.

■ Support locals – buy food and refreshments if they're selling them.

The Top 10
of Everything

Murals at Wat Chalong depicting
scenes from the Buddha's life

TOP 10 Moments in History

Mural depicting the attempted Burmese invasion of 1785

1 1st Century BC– AD 2nd Century: Earliest Records

Phuket was founded by Indian merchants, with trade dating back to the 1st century BC. It was later mentioned by the Greek geographer Ptolemy, who referred to it as "Junk Ceylon," a "cape" en route to the Malaysian peninsula.

2 AD 1500–1700: Tin Seekers

Tin defined Phuket's economy for hundreds of years. The Dutch established a strategic trading presence in Phuket after it was found that the island had vast tin reserves. The English and the French followed shortly after, and the Siamese King Narai (r.1656–88) granted France monopoly in 1685.

3 AD 1688: French Expulsion

After the Siamese revolution of 1688, in which the pro-foreign Siamese King Narai was overthrown, the French were ordered out of Siam (present-day Thailand). The French, under General Marshal Desfarges, captured Phuket in an attempt to reassert influence in Siam in 1689, but the occupation of the island was futile.

4 March 13, 1785: Burmese Invasion Repelled

Led by two sisters – Thao Thep Kasattri and Thao Srisoonthorn – the Siamese defended Phuket against a month-long Burmese attack. Francis Light, an English ship captain, had alerted Phuket of assembling Burmese forces, giving the army time to prepare.

5 Early 19th Century: Chinese Immigration

Lured by Phuket's flourishing tin mines, and to escape poverty in their own country, thousands of Chinese workers immigrated to the island during the early 1800s, establishing communities and customs that define Phuket to the present day. Chinese shrines, architecture, and festivals are among their legacies.

6 1876: Tin Worker Rampage

A group of migrant Chinese tin workers, disgruntled over their low wages and difficult living conditions, instigated a violent uprising on Phuket, causing local residents to flee to Wat Chalong for protection. The monks of the temple sheltered the people and eventually helped restore calm to the island.

7 1933: Phuket Province

During the reign of King Rama V (r.1868–1910), Phuket solidified its role as the administrative center of the southern provinces. The island was, however, only a rural subdivision at the time. It became a full province in 1933.

8 1970s: Arrival of Tourism

Although the island had been a hotbed of international economic activity for centuries, Phuket didn't open to tourism until the 1970s, with the arrival of Western backpackers. Tourism infrastructure, including roads and resorts, was built to cater to island's growing number of visitors, changing the landscape forever.

9 December 26, 2004: Indian Ocean Tsunami

The devastation caused by the tsunami was immense – thousands of lives lost in a matter of minutes. In Thailand, the tsunami represented the worst natural disaster in history, leaving some 8,000 people dead. Busy merchant streets became lethal rapids, and everything on Ko Phi Phi was essentially washed away.

Aftermath of the 2004 tsunami

10 October 13, 2016: Death of King Bhumibol Adulyadej

After a glorious reign of 70 years, Thailand's much revered king, also known as Rama IX, passed away in Bangkok. Remembered for steering the country through many political upheavals, his son, King Vajralongkorn succeeded him.

TOP 10 HISTORICAL FIGURES

Portrait of King Rama V

1 René Charbonneau (17th century)
This French medical missionary once served as the governor of Phuket.

2 Alexandre Chevalier de Chaumont (1640–1710)
France's first ambassador to Siam was granted the country's tin monopoly in 1685.

3 Thao Thep Kasattri (18th century)
This Thai woman and her sister rallied Siamese troops to rise up against the Burmese invasion.

4 Thao Srisoonthorn (18th century)
The Heroines' Monument was built in honor of Thao Srisoonthorn and her sister Thao Thep Kasattri.

5 Captain Francis Light (1740–94)
This British colonial officer alerted the administration in 1785 that Burmese troops were massing for an attack.

6 King Rama V (1853–1910)
Rama V was credited with modernizing Siam and preventing the nation from being colonized by Western powers.

7 Luang Pho Chaem (19th century)
The abbot of Wat Chalong, this monk sheltered local residents during a violent tin worker uprising in 1876.

8 Khaw Sim Bee (1857–1913)
A Chinese immigrant who started the Thai rubber industry, Khaw was made governor of Phuket by Rama V.

9 Mom Luang Tridosyuth Devakul (20th century)
Hotelier and restaurateur, Mom Tri has helped raise Phuket's luxury standards since the 1980s.

10 Pote Sarasin (1905–2000)
The Sarasin Bridge (completed 1967) was named after this Thai politician.

TOP 10 Buddhist Temples

Temple building at Wat Chalong

1 Wat Chalong

Phuket's most visited temple *(see pp16–17)* comprises a number of ornately decorated buildings, which were built at different times. The temple holds statues of former monks and lifelike wax models. Sometimes, there are firecracker displays of gratitude for answered prayers from devotees. The annual Wat Chalong Fair is held at the temple around Chinese New Year.

2 Wat Prathong

Built in the 1750s, and known locally as Wat Phra Phut, this temple *(see p91)* is Phuket's second most important after Wat Chalong. The half-buried golden Buddha statue is the main attraction. According to legend, anyone who tries to uproot the statue will be cursed.

3 Wat Suwan Khiri Khet

MAP H4 ■ Patak Road, Karon ■ Open 8am–5:30pm daily

Also known as Wat Karon because of its location, this temple features engravings depicting scenes from the Buddha's life on the doors and windows. Two fantastic turquoise *naga* serpents encircle the main temple building and form railings down to the entrance. A smaller building guarded by a statue of a yak (a mythical character in *Ramayana* – Thailand's national epic) houses an attractive black sapphire Buddha image.

4 Wat Kathu

MAP J2 ■ Moo 4 Baankathu, Kathu ■ Open 8am–5:30pm daily

Located just outside Patong, this temple offers a peaceful respite from the surrounding frenzy of activity. Its red windows are decorated in gilt-covered reliefs depicting scenes from the Buddha's life; colored glass and tiles decorate the exterior.

5 Wat Suwan Kuha

MAP F2 ■ Phang Nga ■ Open 8am–5:30pm daily

This temple is popularly known as Monkey Temple, for the throngs of pesky animals that reside within its grounds and beg for, or steal, food. The actual Buddhist monuments here are located inside a breath-taking cave, with a massive reclining Buddha image forming the center-piece. Located in Phang Nga, this Buddhist temple is a popular stop for day-trippers from Phuket.

Reclining Buddha of Wat Suwan Kuha

6 Wat Kosit Wihan
MAP K2 ■ Highway 402
■ Open 8am–5:30pm daily

It's a bit of a climb to this temple carved into a hillside, but the reward is great views of Phuket Town. In the grounds stands a large Buddhist cemetery, and a number of small monuments with photographs of the people who were cremated here.

7 Wat Phranang Sang
MAP C5 ■ Thepkasattri Road
■ Open 8am–5pm daily

Built over 200 years ago, Phuket's oldest temple *(see p47)* houses the mummified relics of a former abbot, Luang Poh Bai, and a collection of large tin Buddha images, crafted when tin was still considered a semiprecious metal. The Heroines' Monument stands near this temple.

Temple interior, Wat Phranang Sang

8 Wat Srisoonthorn
MAP C6 ■ Thepkasattri Road
■ Open 7am–5:30pm daily

Towering above this temple is a massive 95-ft- (29-m-) tall reclining Buddha statue, depicting the Buddha as he achieved Enlightenment. Nine other Buddha statues populate the entranceway. Built in 1792, and known locally as Wat Lipon, the temple was later renamed Wat Srisoonthorn to commemorate one of the two sisters *(see p41)* who defended Phuket from Burmese invasion in the 18th century.

9 Wat Putta Mongkol
MAP P5 ■ Dibuk Road, Phuket Town ■ Open 8am–5:30pm daily

Located in the heart of Phuket Town, this temple is sometimes referred to as Wat Klang (literally, central temple). It features colorful architectural designs, including yellow *chedis* (stupas), as well as an old Sino-Portuguese colonial home, which is used as the monks' dormitory. The spacious grounds are also home to the Phuket Buddhist Association and Phuket Old Town Foundation.

10 Wat Kajonrangsan
MAP N5 ■ Ranong Road, Phuket Town ■ Open 7am–5:30pm daily

A unique temple in Phuket Town, Wat Kajonrangsan, also known as Wat Kajon, features distinctive Roman-style architecture in the *ubosot* (ordination chapel). Since Wat Kajonrangsan does not draw busloads of visitors, a visit to the temple also offers a good opportunity to observe an active community environment. The temple grounds also house a school.

🔟 Chinese Shrines

Colorful dragon motifs on the Tha Rua Chinese Shrine

① Tha Rua Chinese Shrine
MAP J1 ▪ Thepkasattri Road
▪ Open 6am–6pm daily

Tha Rua, the largest Chinese temple in Phuket, has undergone a series of massive renovations, reported to cost upward of B40 million and funded entirely by private donations. Colorful, with bold dragon motifs and brightly lit at night, the present Tha Rua Chinese Shrine is far more elaborate in scale than its predecessor.

② Put Jaw Chinese Temple
MAP N5 ▪ Soi Phuthorn, Ranong Road, Phuket Town
▪ Open 6:30am–8pm daily ▪ Adm

The island's oldest Chinese temple is dedicated to the goddess of mercy.

Those suffering from ill-health often come here to pray for relief, and the monks can prescribe Chinese herbal medicines. The temple helps parents name their newborn babies.

③ Kathu Shrine
MAP J2 ▪ Kathu Village
▪ Open 8am–5:30pm daily

Credited as the first Chinese shrine on Phuket to celebrate the annual Vegetarian Festival (see p13), this temple features a fascinating collection of intricately designed Taoist deity statues that are the main objects of worship at the shrine.

④ Boon Kaw Kong Shrine
MAP H2 ▪ Patong Road
▪ Open 9am–5pm daily

Drivers often honk their car horns for good luck as they pass by this revered shrine located on the hilltop between Patong and Kathu. Besides simply hoping for good fortune, the drivers are also acknowledging the ghosts of travelers who have died while passing over the hill in the past. Well integrated in the local community, this small but popular shrine frequently shows films on a giant outdoor screen.

Worshipers, Put Jaw Chinese Temple

⑤ Bang Niew Shrine

MAP Q6 ▪ Ong Sim Phai Road, Phuket Town ▪ Open 7am–5:30pm daily

Built in 1934 and destroyed twice by fire, this shrine – also known as Tao Bong Keng or Chai Tueng – plays a key role in the Vegetarian Festival. Here, one may see devotees with bizarre piercings, or walking across red-hot coals. The shrine houses deities believed to assist worshipers with their career aspirations.

⑥ Sam San Shrine

MAP N5 ▪ Krabi Road, Phuket Town ▪ Open 8am–5:30pm daily

Built in 1853 and dedicated to Mazu, the Chinese goddess of the sea, this shrine frequently hosts ceremonies to consecrate new boats before their maiden sea voyage. The shrine pays homage to the patron saint of sailors, and also features a number of intricate carvings.

⑦ Shrine of the Serene Light

MAP P5 ▪ Chao Fah Nok Road ▪ 07621 1036, 07621 2213 ▪ Open daily

Built by a local Chinese family more than 100 years ago, this historic shrine, once hidden down a narrow alleyway, can be viewed directly from Thalang Road today. Brightly colored ornamentation adorns the roof of the shrine's red-pillared entranceway.

⑧ Cherngtalay Shrine

MAP B6 ▪ Thalang District ▪ Open 7am–5:30pm daily

Popular with local community members who seek healing from the shrine's deities, Cherngtalay Shrine dates back more than 100 years to the founding of a settlement of Chinese tin-mine workers. The ornately decorated tile roof depicts eight immortal Chinese gods, along with the colorful dragon imagery common to many of these temples.

Entrance to Jui Tui Chinese Temple

⑨ Jui Tui Chinese Temple

MAP N5 ▪ Soi Phuthorn, Ranong Road, Phuket Town ▪ Open 8am–8:30pm daily

This colorful Taoist temple, dedicated to the vegetarian deity Kiu Wong In, plays a central role in the Vegetarian Festival. Originally built in 1911 on Soi Romanee, the first Jui Tui temple was destroyed by a fire and rebuilt at its current location.

⑩ Kuan Te Kun Shrine

MAP K1 ▪ Sapam Village ▪ Open 8am–5:30pm daily

Though less prominent, and on a smaller scale, than some of the other shrines on Phuket, Kuan Te Kun – commonly known as Sapam Shrine – is still worth visiting due to its picturesque appearance. With brilliantly colored dragons encircling its four main pillars and guarding its entrance, Kuan Te Kun is full of photo opportunities.

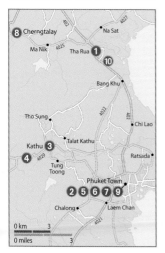

TOP 10 Museums and Monuments

Phuket Mining Museum, housed in a grand mansion

1 Phuket Mining Museum

MAP J2 ▪ Kathu-Ko Kaeo Road, Kathu district ▪ Open 9am–4pm Mon–Sat ▪ Adm

Paying tribute to Phuket's rich tin-mining heritage, this museum has dioramas of early mining techniques, caves, and workers in action. Other exhibits in the Sino-Portuguese style mansion show tin-dredging operations and a model of an opium den.

2 Phuket Seashell Museum

MAP H5 ▪ 12/2 Moo 2, Viset Road, Rawai ▪ 07661 3777 ▪ Open 8am–6pm daily ▪ Adm

Housing a private collection, the Phuket Seashell Museum has more than 2,000 varieties of seashells (see p70), including one weighing 550 lb (250 kg), as well as the world's largest golden pearl.

3 Thai Hua Museum

Originally built to serve as a Thai-Chinese school, this 100-year-old structure today functions as a museum (see p14), exhibition space, and function hall. Visitors can stroll through the old schoolhouse, which has interesting displays depicting daily life during this period.

4 Thalang National Museum

Phuket's national museum (see p92) has a range of displays on the Battle of Thalang, tin mining, the Moken, and the history of the Chinese on Phuket. A magnificent 9th-century Vishnu statue, discovered in the 20th century, stands in the main hall.

5 Saphan Hin Mining Monument

MAP K3 ▪ Near Phuket Town, Phuket Road

Located in a waterfront park, this monument is dedicated to Edward Miles, the Australian ship captain who brought the first tin dredgers to Phuket in 1909.

6 Big Buddha

This 148-ft- (45-m-) tall Buddha (see p82) sits high atop Nakkerd Hill, with sweeping 360-degree views that stretch from Chalong Bay to

Burmese marble Big Buddha

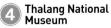

the Andaman Sea. Carved from white Burmese marble, the Buddha *(see p73)* sits cross-legged on a podium decorated with lotus flowers. This is a peaceful, spiritual site.

7 Phuket Philatelic Museum

Dedicated to Thailand's post office, this philately museum *(see p15)* is housed in an 80-year-old 20th-century building in Phuket Town. Old telephones, scales, teletype machines, as well as stamps can be seen here, along with displays on the history of the Thai post office and postal services since its beginnings under King Rama V.

8 Phuket Cultural Centre

This center *(see p13)* has a collection of old artifacts that helps tell the cultural history of Phuket and southern Thailand. Visitors might want to request a guide, since most of the information is in Thai.

Embroidery, Phuket Cultural Centre

9 Thavorn Hotel Lobby Museum

MAP P5 ▪ 74 Rassada Road, Phuket Town ▪ 07621 1333–5

In this magnificent wood-paneled hotel lobby, visitors will discover a fascinating collection of vintage photographs of old Phuket Town and Thai royalty, memorabilia such as classic Thai movie posters, movie projectors, opium pipes, tin-mining equipment, and a range of traditional Chinese wedding hats.

Marigolds on Heroines' Monument

10 Heroines' Monument

Located at the Tha Rua roundabout, unveiled in 1967, this monument *(see p94)* depicts the two sisters who stalled a Burmese invasion *(see p40)* in 1785 by leading women dressed in army uniforms out into the field. The Burmese forces thought that these troops were reinforcements from Bangkok, and withdrew.

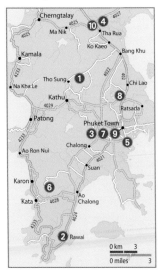

Picturesque Places

1 Ko Phi Phi Leh
With dramatic limestone cliffs giving way to white sand and blue lagoons, this uninhabited island *(see p100)* is a tropical paradise. Day-trippers enjoy snorkeling and swimming in the placid Andaman waters, as well as seeing the 400-year-old wall paintings by fishermen in the Viking Cave. Also visit Maya Bay, where *The Beach* was filmed.

Donald Duck Bay on Ko Similan

2 Similan Islands
One of the top scuba diving destinations in the world, the Similan Islands *(see pp30–31)* are home to rare marine life, including magnificent coral reefs, as well as pristine, unpopulated beaches. Accommodation on overnight snorkeling or diving trips is in tents or very basic bungalows on the beach.

3 Phang Nga Bay
Verdant limestone cliffs jut up from this bay *(see pp36–7)*, with James Bond Island one of the most popular of these land masses. To escape the crowds, look for full-day sea canoe journeys through aquatic grottoes and tunnels.

4 Rang Hill
With sweeping views of Phuket Town and wide expanses of green ideal for picnics, the top of Rang Hill *(see p13)* is one of Phuket's most relaxing spots. People come here to exercise or read a book. Others enjoy the restaurants with magnificent views and the island's best iced coffee. The bronze statue of a former governor stands near the viewpoint.

5 Khao Sok National Park
Beautiful lakes, thrilling caves, and limestone cliffs are interspersed with ancient evergreen trees in this virgin forest north of Phuket. Home to a diverse population of wildlife, as well as rare tree species, Khao Sok *(see pp32–5)* offers some of the best trekking, canoeing, and safaris in southern Thailand.

6 Phromthep Cape
Dramatic, swirling shades of red, purple, and orange appear on the horizon during the sunset crescendo at Phromthep Cape *(see p27)*. The hilltop viewpoint also has restaurants, an outdoor market, an elephant shrine, and a lighthouse.

7 Mangroves
These trees, with their tangled and exposed roots, can be found along Phuket's muddy shorelines. Sea canoe tours offer the best way to see the mangroves up close. They are home to crab-eating macaque monkeys, while underwater they serve as nurseries for crustaceans and fish. The trees themselves are picturesque – and unusual, because they survive in saltwater.

⑧ Sirinat National Park

Located in northwest Phuket, Sirinat National Park (see pp22–3) protects some of Phuket's last mangroves, as well as pristine beaches including Mai Khao Beach, a nesting sites for sea turtles. An elevated nature trail guides visitors through the mangrove forests, with signs explaining the various species.

⑨ Cheow Laan Lake

Surrounded by tree-covered limestone cliffs, this stunning lake (see p32) in the heart of Khao Sok National Park is scattered with floating bamboo-raft houses. In the early morning, the lake's long-tail boats and mist-shrouded shores provide excellent material for photographers. Monkeys, wild boars, and gibbons populate the surrounding forest.

Floating homes on Cheow Laan Lake

⑩ Bang Pae Waterfall

At a height of 59 ft (18 m), this isn't exactly a breathtaking plummet of water, but Bang Pae Waterfall (see p20) offers a picturesque backdrop for swimming. Located close to the Gibbon Rehabilitation Project in the Khao Phra Thaeo Royal Forest and Wildlife Reserve, it is best visited during the rainy season between June and November.

Sailing at Phang Nga Bay

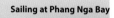

TOP 10 PHUKET VIEWPOINTS

View from Big Buddha

1 Big Buddha Viewpoint
A religious site, this viewpoint (see p82) is home to a massive white marble Buddha statue.

2 Laem Singh Viewpoint
MAP G1
Above the beach of the same name, there is a covered platform with seating.

3 Windmill Viewpoint
MAP H6
A good alternative to the sometimes crowded Phromthep Cape, this vantage point offers great views to the south.

4 Karon Viewpoint
Karon has breathtaking views (see p29) of Kata Noi, Kata, and Karon beaches, plus a sheltered viewing pavilion.

5 Khao Khad Viewing Tower
MAP K4
This hilltop tower in Cape Panwa provides picturesque views, including the Big Buddha statue.

6 Wat Ko Sirey
MAP L3
On an islet off Phuket's east coast, this temple offers great views over the sea.

7 Monkey Hill
Don't get close to the naughty resident macaques on this hill (see p13).

8 Radar Hill Viewpoint
MAP H3
At 1,735 ft (530 m) above sea level, this is the highest point on Phuket.

9 Phi Phi Viewpoint
MAP M5
The route is steep but with good steps. It takes about 30 minutes to reach the top.

10 Helicopter Charters
This is a breathtaking way to see Phuket from above. A ten-minute flight will cost around B5,000.

TOP10 Beaches

Palm-fringed Kata Beach

1 Kata Beach

The seashore here has two separate beaches, Kata Yai and Kata Noi, which are divided by a rocky cliff. Kata Yai is the larger, and busier, of the two. Once a haven for backpackers and hippies, Kata Beach (see pp28–9) today caters to an increasingly upscale crowd, and is very popular for its stunning beauty.

2 Patong Beach

Phuket's premier nightlife center also offers a long, straight beach, ideal for swimming or jogging away the effects of the previous night's revelry. The beach (see pp18–19) has something for everyone: toward the south end, parasailing rides and jet skis roar; moving north, there are sunbeds and umbrellas for rent; while the far north end of the beach is the most peaceful.

3 Bang Tao Beach
MAP B6

Home to international windsurfing competitions, Bang Tao is one of Phuket's best places to catch a wave. The upscale Laguna Phuket Resort complex occupies the middle of the beach, while the northern end is undeveloped, offering a respite from the crowds. You can ride horses on the soft golden sand here for a magical experience.

4 Surin Beach

Populated by numerous high-end resorts, and with expensive private homes on the surrounding hillside, Surin Beach (see p94) is sometimes referred to as Millionaire's Row. The beach is very popular with locals, who appreciate the area's excellent seafood. The water is calm and clear from November to April, but be cautious about strong undertows during the low season.

5 Long Beach
MAP M6

With some of the best beach-access snorkeling on the Ko Phi Phi islands and with breathtaking views of Ko Phi Phi Leh, Long Beach is both secluded and scenic. During the afternoon, it caters almost exclusively to travelers; nights are blissfully quiet.

Long Beach, perfect for snorkeling

The serene Laem Singh Beach

9 Ao Yon Bay
With calm waters and a relaxing ambience, Ao Yon Bay (see p102) is located on the east coast of the island. It is ideal for families with small children, especially when the west coast beaches have high surf. Plenty of good restaurants can also be found here. The Phuket Acquarium (see p60) is situated nearby.

6 Laem Singh Beach
The cliffed coast of Laem Singh Beach (see p92) is one of the island's most beautiful and peaceful beaches. Easily accessible by a quick boat ride from nearby Surin beach, Laem Singh is uncluttered with people. It is perfect for a spot of fun with sunbathing, snorkeling, and swimming.

7 Karon Beach
MAP H4
This large beach offers plenty of space for sunbathers who want a little privacy. With more than 3 miles (5 km) of powdery white sand lapped gently by the turquoise waters of the Andaman Sea, Karon Beach is often less crowded than its neighbors in Patong and Kata. The magnificent coral reef at its southern end is perfect for snorkeling.

8 Mai Khao Beach
Part of Sirinat National Park (see p23), Mai Khao Beach (see p93) is not the usual Phuket tourist beach. There are no private watercraft, and most of the buildings are luxury resorts, none of which infringe on the area's natural beauty. Due to the beach's proximity to the airport, airplanes sometimes fly low overhead. You can also spot sea turtles nesting on the beach.

10 Nai Harn Beach
A quiet beach on Phuket's southwestern tip, Nai Harn beach (see pp26–7) is framed by rolling green hills and emerald waters, and offers a perfect hideaway far from the crowds. The calm, warm water is ideal for swimming, and because there is just one resort property here – the Royal Phuket Yacht Club Hotel, with breathtaking views of the bay – travelers feel as if they've stumbled upon a well-kept secret.

📖10 Scenic Walks

Waterside walk from Nai Harn Beach to Phromthep Cape

1 Nai Harn Beach to Phromthep Cape

Walk away from the beach, head clockwise around Nai Harn Lake, and follow signs to Phromthep Cape. The hilly, stretching walk will take you past Yanui Beach. At the end of the path are two awesome viewpoints – one facing Nai Harn Beach (see pp26–7), and the other, westward over the Andaman Sea.

2 Similan Islands

Best known for its exciting underwater sites, the Similan Islands (see pp30–31) also offer a few hiking trails. On Ko Similan, the main island, a tree-lined path winds up to a viewpoint with breathtaking vistas. The best part, of course, is that you'll see hardly a soul on your way up.

3 Khao Lak

A number of hiking trails can be found in and around Khao Lak (see p100), including a popular scenic forest path starting near the base of the 33-ft- (10-m-) tall Chong Fah Waterfall. Sturdy shoes help when walking the rough jungle trails here.

Buddhist monks once kept forest retreats in the area; the ruins of these shelters can still be seen.

4 Khao Sok National Park

Trek through ancient forest in Khao Sok (see pp32–5), encountering birds, wildlife, and orchids. Keen bird-watchers will be delighted to see several species of hornbill, while long-tail macaque monkeys and gibbons swing through the trees above. Paddle Asia (see p33) offers a popular soft adventure tour for spotting wildlife, as well as tailored trips.

Hornbill at Khao Sok

5 Surin Beach to Kamala

From ritzy Surin Beach, home to top-end resort properties, walk south along the sand until you reach a pathway crossing over to Laem Singh Beach (see p51). This stunningly picturesque cape on the west coast is tucked between Surin and Kamala. Spend some time here before continuing to Kamala, where there is a relaxed beach and fishing village.

6 Chinese Shrines in Phuket Town

A popular way to enjoy the sights of Phuket Town is to focus on its wonderful markets and colorful Chinese shrines. Jui Tui and Put Jaw, two of Phuket's most important Chinese shrines, are located near Ranong Road. This walking tour is marked on the Phuket Town Historical Map, distributed free at Phuket International Airport.

7 Mangrove Forests on Mai Khao Beach

At the northern end of Mai Khao Beach *(see p23)* stands one of Phuket's most pristine mangrove forests. An elevated walkway guides visitors above these fascinating trees, which survive in saltwater. Signs describe the plant species here, which include black myrsina, red cycas, and mountain ebony.

Phuket Town's historic achitecture

8 Historical Architecture in Phuket Town

Take a walk back in time past the classic homes and shops built during Phuket's tin boom in the late 19th and early 20th centuries *(see pp14–15)*. Many were constructed in the Sino-Portuguese architectural style. The best routes to take are down Phang Nga, Thalang, Dibuk, Krabi, and Yaowarat roads. Keep an eye out for the spectacular Soi Romanee, located off Thalang Road.

9 Patong

Begin this stroll from the southern end of Patong Beach *(see p18)* around dusk. As you walk up the main beach road, you'll pass by bustling open-air restaurants displaying the day's catch on ice, and lively cocktail-sipping crowds. Turn right onto hedonistic Bangla Road *(see p19)* and spend some time simply people-watching.

10 Khao Phra Thaeo Royal Forest and Wildlife Reserve

The most popular trek in this national park *(see pp20–21)* begins at the park headquarters at Ton Sai Waterfall, navigates through 4 miles (6 km) of virgin forest, and ends at Bang Pae Waterfall. Besides abundant natural plant species, the park is also home to monkeys, flying foxes, wild pigs, and cobras.

Lush forests of Khao Phra Thaeo

Outdoor Activities

① Tai Chi and Qi Gong
These ancient Chinese practices, although based on martial arts, are not violent, and more akin to yoga or meditation. Classes are available, but once you're more skilled, you can join the morning sessions in the Suan Luang Park *(see p13)* in Phuket town.

② Motorbike Rides
Cruise the hilly coastal roads of western Phuket, past scenic viewpoints and tropical foliage, on your bike. Inexperienced riders should be cautious, as the roads are winding and other drivers are often careless.

Rock climbing on Tonsai Tower

③ Rock Climbing
Gecko Extreme Adventure: 091 325 4958; www.gecko thailand.com
With more than 30 climbing routes, Tonsai Tower on Ko Phi Phi Don *(see p101)* has a number of easy routes which make it ideal for beginners. Visitors can also find a range of rock climbing options on Phang Nga Bay *(see pp36–7)*.

Horseback riding on the beach

④ Horseback Riding
Phuket Riding Club: MAP C5; 60/9 Thepkasattri Road, Thalang; 081 787 2455; www.phuketridingclub.com
Mornings and late afternoon are the best time to saddle up for a horseback ride, since midday can be very hot.

⑤ ATV Touring
59/26 Moo 5, T. Srisuntorn A. Thalang; 089 874 0055; www.atv phuket.com
All-terrain vehicles are an exciting way to see local villages, farms, and off-the-beaten-path sights. Phuket ATV Tour includes an option to go white-water rafting in Phang Nga, or to experience a ropes course. Wear sports clothes and closed-toe shoes.

⑥ Trekking
Thailand's scenic jungle paths lead hikers past waterfalls and lush flora, full of wild orchids and ferns. The Khao Phra Thaeo Royal Forest and Wildlife Reserve *(see pp20–21)* has a scenic trail and at Khao Sok National Park *(see pp32–5)* walkers can trek through luxuriant jungle and beautiful bamboo forests.

7 Cycling

Bike Tours Thailand: 07626 3575; www.biketoursthailand.com

Cycling through Phuket's beautiful countryside is a great way to explore and to get some exercise while on holiday. Half-day, full-day, and overnight tours through breath-taking scenery also allow cyclists to meet locals.

8 Paragliding

Paragliding Phuket: MAP H5; Karon Beach; 07877 2320; www.para glidingphuket.com

Those seeking an adrenaline fix can soar through the air on an incredible paragliding experience above Karon Beach. There's no better way to get a bird's-eye view of the coastal landscape.

9 Ziplining

Hanuman World: MAP J4; 105 Moo 4 Chaofah Road, Wichit; 062 979 5533; www.hanumanworld phuket.com

Safely strapped into a harness and attached to a cable, zipliners sail high above ground propelled only by gravity. Phuket has several zipline providers.

10 Golf

Phuket is one of Thailand's top golfing destinations, thanks to its picturesque and challenging courses. The rolling greens of the Blue Canyon Country Club's (see p92) two championship courses host a number of professional golf tour events that attract acclaimed golfers.

Blue Canyon golf course

TOP 10 ACTIVITIES FOR RAINY DAYS

Indulge in a Thai massage

1 Thai Massage
This ultra-relaxing form of massage involves stretching and deep, but not painful, pressure.

2 Cooking Classes
Learn to make delicious traditional Thai food at one of the island's many local cooking schools.

3 Spa Treatment
With its legendary hospitality, Thailand has earned a reputation as one of Asia's top spa destinations.

4 Museums
Phuket's rich tin-mining history can be seen through exhibits at a number of local cultural museums.

5 Temples
Visit one of Phuket's 40 Buddhist temples to observe local monks performing traditional ceremonies.

6 Batik Painting Class
Visit a batik gallery and create your own version of the popular southeast Asian fabric art.

7 Shopping
Rain or shine, the street markets are always open. Phuket has many indoor shopping complexes too.

8 Gaming
Patong's Game Space (see p60) is an entertainment complex offering laser tag as well as arcade and virtual games.

9 Cinema
SF Cinema City, located at Jungceylon in Patong, and the cinemas at Central Festival near Phuket Town, all show the latest releases.

10 Bowling
A modern bowling alley with 16 lanes is located at SF Cinema City.

🔟 Marine Activities

Snorkeling in Phuket's azure waters

① Snorkeling
Almost every beach here has snorkeling opportunities, with boat trips to the popular shallow-water reefs surrounding Phuket. Masks, fins, and snorkels are available at beachfront rental shops.

② Kite Surfing
Kite Boarding Asia: MAP B4; 74/10 Nai Yang Beach (Dec–Mar: MAP J4; Chalong Bay); 087 082 3058; www.kiteboardingasia.com
The northern beaches of Phuket get the best wind for this activity, in which a parachute-like kite pulls the rider on a small surfboard. Since a level of skill is required, it can be more rewarding than parasailing.

Kayakers at Phang Nga Bay

③ Swimming
A translucent turquoise, delightfully warm, and fringed by soft sand, the Andaman Sea has made Phuket one of the world's favorite destinations. Whether at bustling Patong or idyllic Yanui, Phuket's beaches offer great swimming.

④ Deep-Sea Fishing
Phuket Fishing Charters: MAP J4; 48/12 Soi Sunrise, Chalong; 062 060 0220; www.phuketfishing charters.com
The Andaman Sea offers anglers a chance to cast for big-game fish, from prized marlins and sailfish to hard-fighting tuna and giant trevally. Most sportfishing off Phuket operates on a catch-and-release policy.

⑤ Scuba Diving
The dive sites here are among the best in the world. With crystal-clear visibility, gorgeous coral reefs and rock formations, and abundant sea life, there are astonishing underwater opportunities for divers.

⑥ Kayaking
Explore Phang Nga Bay's extraordinary sea caves in a kayak or a canoe. Rock tunnels lead into lagoons surrounded by jungles with hornbills, kingfishers, and even monkeys. John Gray's Sea Canoe (see p37) has been leading eco-friendly canoe trips since 1983.

7 Surfing

Though not one of the world's main surfing destinations, Phuket's west coast nonetheless offers ample opportunities to catch a wave. Kata and Bangtao beaches host annual surfing and windsurfing competitions. Other surf spots include Kalim, Nai Harn, and Surin beaches.

8 Parasailing

As the speedboat accelerates, your parachute pulls you up into the sky to enjoy staggering overhead views of emerald waters and green hills. Once the excitement of takeoff is over, you'll soon feel relaxed while surveying the scene below.

Sailing on a traditional junk

9 Sailing

Phuket Sail Tours: MAP C5; Ao Por Centre, 80/17, 18 Moo 6, Pakhlok, Thalang; 087 897 0492; www.phuket sailtours.com

Cruise to uninhabited islands with pearly sand beaches, palm trees, and blue waters. Chartered yacht, sailboat, and junk trips offer an opportunity to explore unspoiled locations in the Andaman Sea.

10 Phuket Wake Park

MAP J2 ■ Phuket Cable Ski, 86/3 Moo 6, Vichitsongkram Road, Kathu ■ 08987 30187 ■ Open 9:30am–sundown daily ■ www.phuketwake park.com

Since 1997, Phuket's only wake park has given wakeboarders and water skiers a setting to hone their skills, with ramps, kickers, and slide rails.

TOP 10 BIG GAME FISH IN PHUKET

Grouper swimming among coral

1 Grouper
The biggest grouper ever caught off Phuket, captured with shark bait, weighed nearly 198 lb (90 kg).

2 Yellow Fin Tuna
These beautiful, powerful fish have long been one of the favorite prey of big-game anglers.

3 Dogtooth Tuna
These massive fish dwell near elevated tropical reef pinnacles in the deep waters around Phuket.

4 Dorado
Sometimes called mahi-mahi, these surface-dwelling, ray-finned fish are fantastically colorful.

5 Giant Trevally
Though not physically huge, the giant trevally puts up one of the toughest fights in the sea.

6 Wahoo
The meat of the wahoo, a prized big-game fish, is considered a delicacy by many gourmet cooks.

7 Spanish Mackerel
With its razor-sharp teeth, this fish often cuts its way through trolling bait.

8 Barracuda
This toothy, ray-finned fish eats almost everything. It is well known for its frightening appearance.

9 Black Marlin
One of the most prized captures in the Asia Pacific, the black marlin makes for the perfect trophy.

10 Sailfish
The ocean's fastest fish migrates through waters near Phuket during the summer months.

Following pages *Performance at the famous Simon Cabaret at Patong Beach, Phuket*

⑩ Children's Attractions

Elephants under the canopy walkway, Phuket Elephant Sanctuary

① Phuket Elephant Sanctuary
MAP P5 ■ 100 Moo 2, Paklok, Thalang Road ■ 088 752 3853 ■ Open 9:30am–5pm daily ■ Adm ■ www.phuket elephantsanctuary.org

This ethical elephant sanctuary is home to several animals rescued from the tourism and logging industries. It features a long canopy walkway from which visitors can observe the elephants in their natural environment. It's a fun and memorable educational experience for all the family.

② Game Space
MAP N2 ■ 29/1 Bangla Road, Patong ■ 07634 4193 ■ Open 2pm–12:30am daily ■ www.gamespace laserbattle.com

Laser tag, arcade games, and virtual reality adventures keep the whole family entertained for hours here. It's one of the only family-friendly spaces on Bangla Road.

③ Phuket Aquarium
Set on a scenic bay, this aquarium is a part of the Phuket Marina Biological Center. Phuket Aquarium *(see p84)* houses over 150 fresh- and saltwater species, including electric eels, sharks, sea turtles, and stingrays. Displays cover Thailand's rivers, lakes, coral reefs, and mangroves.

④ Surf House
Kata Beach: MAP H5; Southern Kata Beach; 08197 97737; open 10am–midnight daily ■ Patong Beach: MAP N2; 162/6-7 Taweewong Road; 08815 61555; open 9:30am–11pm daily ■ Adm ■ www.surfhousephuket.com

A high-pressure wave-generating machine throws a shallow sheet of water up a sloping "pool." Beginner surfers hold onto a safety rope. If they should happen to "wipe out," the water flow ensures that, instead of sliding back down, they shoot safely upward. It's great fun for kids over 10.

⑤ Splash Jungle Waterpark
With twisting waterslides, a wave pool, and the 1,100-ft- (335-m-)

Slides at the Splash Jungle Waterpark

long lazy river, this water-theme park (see p94) is excellent. In the Boomerango water slide you will plunge down, through a tube, into the Super Bowl, before hitting the splashdown pool.

6 Go Karting
MAP H2 ▪ Patong Go-Kart Speedway, 118/5 Vichitsongkram Road, Kathu ▪ 07632 1949 ▪ Open 10am–7pm daily ▪ Adm ▪ www.gokartthailand.com

With kids' karts reaching speeds up to 25 mph (40 kmph), and specially designed karts driven by an adult with a child's passenger seat, this place often hosts Mini Grand Prix races, including competitions for kids.

Golfing with dinosaurs at Dino Park

7 Mini-Golf at Dino Park
MAP H4 ▪ Marina Phuket Resort, Karon Beach ▪ 07633 0625 ▪ Open 10am–11pm daily ▪ Adm ▪ www.dinopark.com

This 18-hole miniature golf course navigates around a swamp, lava cave, waterfall, erupting volcano, and a roaring Tyrannosaurus Rex. A fun environment for a competitive round of putting, it also has a theme bar and restaurant.

8 The Kids Club
MAP N2 ▪ 2nd floor, Kee Shopping Plaza, 152/1 Thaewong Road ▪ 081 085 0008 ▪ Open 10am–9pm daily ▪ Adm

The Kids Club offers slides, crawl tubes, swings, a trampoline, a ball room, a flying fox ride, an indoor

soccer pitch, and much more for children of all ages. On duty, there are seven full-time nannies, who assure the play stays fun and safe.

9 Upside Down House
MAP K1 ▪ Bypass Road, near Siam Niramit, Phuket Town ▪ 07637 6245 ▪ Open 10am–6pm daily ▪ Adm

A pleasant two-story family home that, as the name implies, stands on its head. Enter through the attic, work your way "up" or "down to the bottom", to walk on the ceiling or gaze up at the fully furnished house including the living room and the bedrooms. The quirky set up provides a fun photo opportunity and can keep the children entertained for hours as they explore the Upside Down House. There is also an outdoor maze garden as well as a secret escape room.

10 Blue Tree
MAP B6 ▪ 4/2 Srisoonthorn Road, Cherngtalay ▪ 07669 2435 ▪ Open 10am–10pm daily ▪ Adm ▪ www.bluetree.fun

This waterpark has everything you need for a day of fun under the sun: water slides, paddleboards, ziplines, and cliff jumps.

Entertainment Venues

1 Beach Clubs
Some of Thailand's best parties take place at Phuket's beach clubs. You can groove to local and international DJ sets, taking breaks to dip your toes in the ocean and watch the fire shows. Top clubs include Baba near Natai Beach, Café Del Mar (see p65), Kudo on Patong Beach (see p85), and Catch on Bang Tao Beach.

2 Bangla Boxing Stadium
The upper deck seats at Bangla Boxing Stadium (see p18) look straight down at the action, and are close enough that an uppercut glancing off a boxer's jaw might make you leap out of your seat. These are the best seats in the house. Fight promoters cruise through the streets of Patong in pickup trucks during the afternoon, promoting the fights of the day with loud Muay Thai music.

3 Simon Star Show
MAP J4 ■ Near Central Festival
■ 076 523 1926 ■ Open from 5:30pm
■ www.simonstarshow.com
Phuket's most popular cabaret, wild but family friendly, features outrageous costumes and sets, along with a flamboyant cast of drag performers. Since 1991, Simon Cabaret (see p18) in Patong has offered state of the art sound and lighting, as well as extravagance. This show, the latest branch, is a convenient option for visitors staying near Phuket town.

Flamboyant Simon Cabaret

Bangla Road's nightlife scene

4 Bangla Road
MAP N2
For people-watching, you won't find a setting more outrageous than the night scene on the infamous Bangla Road. At once seedy and harmless, this central vein of Patong is filled with beer bars, club promoters, and pleasure-seeking travelers from every corner of the globe. The streets coming off Bangla Road are home to even more entertainment venues.

5 Phuket Fantasea
A spectacular stage show (see p82) stars trapeze artists and traditional dancers.There's also a theme park filled with games and shops, all with an elephant theme.

6 Ka Jok See
Much more than just a restaurant that serves great Thai food, Ka Jok See (see p86) combines dining and entertainment. Post-dinner, guests are given bongo drums and tambourines while the staff give a riotous cabaret performance. Reservations are recommended.

7 Phuket Siam Niramit
MAP K2 ▪ Chalermprakiet Road, Ratsada, north of Phuket Town ▪ 07633 5000 ▪ Open 5:30–10:30pm Wed–Mon ▪ www.siamniramit.com

A tasteful but lively cultural showcase of the best of Thai classical dance, music, and martial arts, with top-level performers and special effects. The show itself runs from 8:30–10pm, but it's best to arrive early to enjoy the Thai village, and floating market on the grounds. Good for the whole family.

8 Patong Boxing Stadium
Phuket's top venue (see p18) to watch Muay Thai presents real fights every Monday and Thursday night. Foreigners who train at the local gyms frequently get onto the cards against each other, or local Thai boxers, and these fights are often among the most exciting. Early evening fights pit younger, lightweight boxers against one another; the bouts gradually build up toward the main event.

Muay Thai, Patong Stadium

9 Fire Dancing
A popular sight in most clubs, and some beaches and hotels, fire dancing features flaming staffs and poi spinning in the darkness to pulsating music. To watch these glowing rays of light is mesmerizing, and in photographs the fire dancers often appear to be playing with halos.

10 LGBTQ+ Venues
Phuket is home to some excellent gay bars, where members of the LGBTQ+ community can catch drag performances and cabaret acts, or dance the night away. Two of the best options in Patong are Zag Club and My Way.

TOP 10 FILMS SHOT IN PHUKET

The Man with the Golden Gun

1 *The Man with the Golden Gun* **(1974)**
This 007 movie featured Ko Khao Phing Kan (see p36), now popularly known as James Bond Island.

2 *The Killing Fields* **(1984)**
Based on Cambodia's Khmer Rouge regime, this movie shows Phuket's French and US embassies.

3 *Good Morning, Vietnam* **(1987)**
Starring Robin Williams and Chintara Sukapatana, this film's jungle scenes were shot in Phuket.

4 *Casualties of War* **(1989)**
Brian De Palma's Vietnam War film features very realistic jungle scenes filmed in Phuket.

5 *Cutthroat Island* **(1995)**
Starring Geena Davis, this pirate film was shot in secluded Maya Bay on Ko Phi Phi Leh (see p100).

6 *Tomorrow Never Dies* **(1997)**
Phang Nga Bay (see p36–7) was portrayed as Vietnam's Halong Bay in this 007 film.

7 *The Beach* **(2000)**
Ko Phi Phi Leh's Maya Bay stole the show in this movie by Danny Boyle.

8 *Star Wars: Episode III – Revenge of the Sith* **(2005)**
Backdrops from Krabi province were featured in this movie.

9 *The Impossible* **(2012)**
Shot and set in Khao Lak, this movie is based on the true story of a Spanish family caught up in the 2004 tsunami.

10 *Patong Girl* **(2014)**
This film follows a German family's visit to Phuket, where the teenage son falls in love with a transgender Thai woman.

🔟 Bars and Nightclubs

Musicians playing a gig at the Timber Hut

1 Timber Hut

Phuket Town's top live music venue *(see p85)* features an excellent in-house band. Busy during the week, and sometimes downright wild on weekends, this is a great place to dance and party. A favorite with local Thais, the bar also attracts its fair share of foreign visitors.

2 After Beach Bar

Near Karon Viewpoint, on the winding mountain road between Kata and Rawai, this relaxing bar *(see p85)* overlooking the sea plays a constant stream of reggae and acoustic tunes. It's popular for post-beach cocktails while watching the sunset.

3 Rockin' Angels Blues Café

MAP P4 ▪ 55 Yaowarat Road, Old Phuket Town ▪ 89654 9654 ▪ Closed Mon

This lively blues venue is run by a Singaporean guitarist. The café and bar may be small, but it is a great place to hang out if you become tired of the blaring dance music heard elsewhere in the town. There are live blues and classic rock performances from the band six nights a week.

4 Patong Bay Hill

House-party vibes prevail at this resort *(see p85)*. During the day, revelers hit the pool area for waterside boogying. Come nighttime, many of the hotels' rooms are turned into impromptu nightclubs, each playing different music. Bars are even set up in the hallways between rooms. Rent one of the suites to party all night long.

5 Sunflower Beach Bar

MAP M6 ▪ Tonsai, Ko Phi Phi ▪ Open 11am–11pm ▪ 08003 83374

Sunflower is more relaxed than most Tonsai nightlife. The "buckets" (Thai whiskey, Red Bull, cola and ice, in a plastic bucket) are infamous, but it offers coconut-based cocktails, too.

Selection of drinks, After Beach Bar

6 Z1implex Mixology Laboratory

MAP Q5 ▪ Phang Nga Road ▪ 084 003 6664 ▪ Open 8–12pm daily

Unique, friendly, trendy – this Phuket venue is comfortable and cozy, with a DJ that keeps the volume at the right level for conversation.

7 Kee Sky Lounge

A sophisticated place to spend an evening, Kee Sky Lounge (see p85) has a nautical theme, complete with a wooden deck, sun loungers and a panoramic view of the sea. It serves excellent food as well as drinks.

8 Illuzion Nightclub

Highly popular, Illuzion Nighclub (see p85) features a range of entertainment including international DJs, live acts, hip-hop shows and underground sets. It can hold upto 5,000 people and hosts globally famous artists.

Live DJ performance at Illuzion

9 Café Del Mar

This beach club (see p85) hosts some of the world's best DJs. It has a dance floor, a pool with floaties, a restaurant serving sushi and Thai dishes, and chill-out booths where you can catch your breath.

10 Molly's Tavern

The island's most popular Irish pub has been going strong since it first opened in 1999. On the main beach road, Molly's Tavern (see p85) offers live pub-rock every night, and flatscreen TVs broadcast live sports. It serves traditional pub fare, as well as brews such as Guinness, Kilkenny, and Magners Cider on tap.

TOP 10 FAVORITE LOCAL DRINKS

Singha and Chang beers

1 Singha Beer
Most foreigners pronounce the name of this lager as "Singh-ha," although the proper pronunciation is "Singh."

2 Chang Beer
This potent lager is one of the country's top-selling beers. Equally popular on tourist T-shirts is the Chang elephant logo.

3 Leo Beer
A flavorful lager, Leo Beer is produced by Boon Rawd Breweries.

4 Tiger Beer
Singapore's first locally brewed beer is popular throughout Thailand.

5 Red Bull Cocktails
The energy drink's formula was invented by a Thai businessman, who still owns 49 per cent of the company.

6 "Buckets"
Be wary of this potent Thai specialty, a mix of alcohol, cola, and Red Bull in a bucket, meant to serve a group.

7 Sang Som
Despite its reputation as a Thai whiskey, the liquor is in fact a rum.

8 Phuket Beer
The bottle's logo features a brightly colored hornbill, perched near Phuket's Phromthep Cape.

9 100 Pipers
This popular western-style whiskey is imported from (although not bottled in) Scotland.

10 San Miguel Light
This brew from the Philippines can be found widely throughout Thailand, including Phuket.

Restaurants

① Silk
A stylish Thai restaurant with contemporary interiors, Silk (see p87) serves some of the best Thai cuisine in Phuket. The snapper in ginger, celery and pickled plums is a must-try as is the signature "dish, the Goon Sarong, with prawns wrapped in Phuket noodles.

② The Boathouse Restaurant
This stylish seaside restaurant (see p87) features a huge wine cellar with more than 800 labels. The excellent French and Thai fusion cuisine competes with classic grill favorites, such as prime meat and chops.

③ Suay
Superstar local chef Noi Tammasak has given Thai food a contemporary twist at this excellent Cherngtalay restaurant (see p97). Expect picture-perfect dishes, lots of spices, and a stylish setting. The restaurant also hosts various live music events on Mondays and Thursdays. On weekends, it offers fresh seafood dishes.

Stylish White Box Restaurant

④ White Box Restaurant
With a rooftop lounge with stunning views of Patong Bay, this Mediterranean- and Thai-inspired restaurant (see p87) is popular for cocktails and tapas. In-house jazz musicians, as well as global DJs, entertain diners from 10pm.

⑤ Thong Dee Brasserie
A top-quality and well-priced restaurant, Thong-Dee (see p87) serves international and Thai cuisine. The Khi Mao spaghetti is a creative fusion of Thai and Italian, while the Australian tenderloin is a real treat.

⑥ On the Rock
Diners could not be any closer to the sea at this highly acclaimed restaurant (see p87), which is part of the Marina Phuket Resort. Much of the attraction is the ambience created by the views offered thanks to the restaurant's position on Karon Beach (see p51). To be seated at a beachfront table, particularly for sunset, often requires a reservation well in advance. The seaside setting is reflected in On the Rock's seafood menu.

Elegant interiors at Suay

7 Ka Jok See

Tucked into an 18th-century Sino-Portuguese shop house in Phuket Town, this charming restaurant *(see p86)*, with exposed wooden beams and candlelit tables, serves delicious traditional Thai cuisine. However, the night really begins after dessert, when the music is cranked up for one of Ka Jok See's legendary dance parties. Reservations are recommended.

8 Baan Rim Pa

Perched on a cliff above Kalim and Patong bays, Baan Rim Pa *(see p87)* serves royal Thai cuisine, once found only in the kingdom's palaces. The emphasis in this cooking is on precise presentation and color, so it requires special training for chefs.

Baan Rim Pa's dramatic setting

9 Sala Bua

Located at Impiana Cabana Resort *(see p113)*, this beachfront restaurant *(see p87)* features Thai and Pacific-Rim fusion cuisine. The Australian fire-roasted Chateaubriand is recommended.

10 Kopitiam by Wilai

Serving *hokkien mee* (Hokkien fried noodles), a Phuket specialty, this colorful restaurant *(see p86)* is the younger sibling of the perennially popular Wilai restaurant. The space has been designed like a Chinese shop house. Other specialties include *phat thai* and southern Thai curries.

TOP 10 THAI DISHES

Khao niaw mamuang **dessert**

1 Khao Niaw Mamuang
Made with succulent fresh mango and sticky rice, this dish is drizzled with a sweet coconut cream sauce.

2 Phat Thai
An iconic Thai street food, this features stir-fried rice noodles, eggs, fish sauce, tamarind juice, and more.

3 Phat Kraprao
This spicy, flavorful stir-fry is made with chili and basil leaves, and is often served with rice and a fried egg.

4 Gaeng Kiaw Wan
A Thai green curry, this dish is usually cooked with chicken or beef, and can be spicy and a little sweet.

5 Gai Phat Met Mamuang
Chicken stir-fried with cashew nuts is a popular Thai dish, especially in tourist areas.

6 Somtam
A spicy salad made from shredded unripened papaya, *somtam* is often eaten with sticky rice.

7 Tom Kha Gai
Made with coconut milk, galangal, lemongrass, and chicken, this is a delicious hot soup.

8 Khao Phat
A simple dish made of Thai fried rice, *khao phat* is often served with cucumber and sweet chili sauce.

9 Por Pia
These Thai spring rolls, usually fried, are often stuffed with vegetables, noodles, and pork or shrimp.

10 Tom Yum Gung
Simmered in a clear broth, this hot and sour prawn soup is a crowd-pleaser.

TOP 10 Markets and Shopping Areas

1 Jungceylon
MAP P2 ■ Open 11am–11pm daily ■ www.jungceylon.com

Anchored by a department store and a French supermarket, Jungceylon – a massive international mall in Patong – has over 300 shops selling everything from sports clothes to perfumes and luxury cosmetics.

Exterior space at Jungceylon

2 Central Festival Phuket
MAP J3 ■ Open 10:30am–10pm daily

Central, Thailand's top retailer, runs the biggest mall on the island. Featuring a department store, over 120 outlets, good restaurants, and cinemas, this mall was made even larger by Central Floresta during a 2018 expansion.

3 Thalong and Dibuk Roads
MAP P5

These streets in old Phuket Town offer many wonderful shops tucked inside historical buildings selling Chinese embroidery, antiques, wooden figurines, and products from Laos, Cambodia, and Myanmar.

4 Phromthep Cape Market
The best souvenirs from this popular viewpoint (see p27) might be your own photos, but you'll also find a wide range of handicrafts and original artwork in the cape's outdoor markets. Arrive in the late afternoon, before the crowds start pouring in.

5 Naka Weekend Market
This large, open-air bazaar (see p12) sells soaps, candles, sculpture, beachwear, flip-flops, used shoes, and almost anything else you can imagine. It also has dozens of stands selling Thai food.

6 Boat Avenue
MAP C5

This lively area of Cherngtalay is known for its fashion boutiques and upscale restaurants. It also has a Friday night market (see p96), which spills from brightly colored shipping containers onto the street.

7 Phuket Art Village
MAP H5 ■ 2 Soi Naya, Rawai

Take a stroll in the homey studio galleries that make up this art collective to find the perfect piece for your home. If you're lucky, you'll be able to speak to the artists themselves about their work.

8 Phuket Town Night Market
MAP P5

With lower prices than in Patong, Kata, and Karon, the night market on Thalang Road, in Phuket Town, offers a similar selection of T-shirts, fishermen's pants, and wood-carvings, as well as second-hand clothes and Thai music albums.

Patong night market's food stalls

9 Patong Night Market

At sundown, vendors throughout Phuket set up makeshift tables and tents to peddle everything from handicrafts to DVDs. Patong's night market (see p19) in particular turns the entire town into one big, sprawling night bazaar.

10 Plaza Surin

MAP A6 ■ Open 9am–8pm daily

For high-end boutiques, visit Plaza Surin's 12 stores, which sell unique items, such as Thai furnishings, original artwork, natural spa products, and cutting-edge audio-visual goods. The upscale Silk (see p66), is a restaurant and bar serving delicious Thai cuisine.

Phuket Town's lively night market

TOP 10 FRUITS IN PHUKET

1 Mangosteen
The thick, red skin of this fruit (mang khut) encloses sweet, slightly tart, and creamy white segments inside.

2 Mango
No Thai holiday is complete without trying sweet mango (ma muang) with sticky rice.

3 Lychee
A major Thai export, the lychee (lin jee) has a thin, hard skin that encloses a thick layer of sweet flesh surrounding a small seed.

4 Longan
Covered with a crisp skin, this fruit (lam yai) has sweet flesh that resembles that of a lychee.

5 Rose Apple
This decorative bell-shaped fruit (chompoo) has glossy pink skin, with crisp, juicy, and acidic flesh inside.

6 Durian
The world's smelliest fruit, durian is not permitted inside some hotels. The creamy yellow flesh inside the spiky shell is considered an acquired taste.

7 Papaya
This is a staple fruit in the Thai diet. Try the spicy green papaya salad (som tam) for a fiery experience.

8 Pomelo
Somewhat like an Asian grapefruit, this citrus fruit (som oh) features in the excellent Thai salad yam som oh.

9 Rambutan
A very interesting-looking fruit, the rambutan (ngo) features a hairy red exterior covering soft, sweet, oval-shaped flesh.

10 Dragon Fruit
This wonderful pink fruit (geow mangon) is shaped like a flower and has light, sweet, and crunchy flesh.

Fragrant, sweet dragon fruit

Souvenirs

Interior of Chan's Antique House

4 Local Crafts
OTOP Shopping Paradise: MAP N2; Rat U Thit 200 Pee Road, Kathu, Phuket
Revenues from sales are passed directly to the crafts people, so the market provides local and rural artisans with a better income.

5 Religious Amulets
MAP P5
The best selection of religious items is found in the Amulet Market in the center of old Phuket Town. While mainly Buddhist, Taoist and animist pieces are also on offer, and are taken seriously by aficionados; rare and, supposedly, powerful pieces can fetch prices upward of B100,000.

1 Antiques
Chan's Antique House: MAP J2; 99/42, Moo 5, Chalermprakiat, Ratchakan Thi 9 Road; www.chans-antique.com
The best places for genuine antiques are Soul of Asia (see p95), an art gallery housed in two old Chinese shops, and upscale Chan's Antique House, which offers Phuket's largest collection of art and antiques.

2 Seashells
The Phuket Seashell Museum (see p46) is the best place for rare seashells or seashell handicrafts. The Phromthep Cape market (see p68) also offers a great selection.

3 Bespoke Clothing
Phuket's bespoke tailors are commonly found in Patong, Kata, and Karon beaches. Don't wait until the end of your trip; several fittings are needed. They can also copy any garment you bring to the shop. Pay attention to the fabric quality used, and avoid shops with streetside touts.

6 Original Artwork
Artists sell original paintings and reproductions at street-side galleries throughout Phuket. The quality varies, and the costs are always negotiable.

Vibrant Thai silk cushions

7 Thai Silk
Jim Thompson: www.jimthompson.com
Thai silk is not as fine as the Chinese variety, but it is lustrous and hangs well in clothing. The best source is Jim Thompson, named for the American tycoon who revived, and later epitomized, the Thai silk industry. There are six branches on Phuket, including one at the airport.

⑧ Traditional Thai Furniture

Island Furniture: MAP J3; 90/4 Moo 2, Chao Fah West Road; 07626 3707; www.islandfurniture-phuket.com
Furniture made of crushed bamboo, recovered teak wood, rattan, water hyacinth, and more can be found in many shops. Island Furniture can recreate pieces from sketches or from photographs.

⑨ Batik Cloth

Although an Indonesian craft, Phuket artisans are now using this wax-resist dyeing technique and incorporating Thai artistic motifs. Cloth and items made from it are easy to find in boutiques and night markets. Look for the government-sponsored OTOP brand pieces.

Colorful Thai Batik cloth for sale

⑩ Pearls

Phuket Pearl Factory: MAP K1; 58/2 Moo 1, Tambon Kohkaew; 07623 8002; www.phuketpearl.com
White, black, or cream pearls, produced on local pearl farms, can be found in Phuket's markets. You can see how pearls are cultured and extracted at Naka Noi island, off the northeastern coast.

Farmed pearls being selected

TOP 10 BARGAINING TIPS

Market traders, Phuket

1 Have fun
Approach your shopping experience lightheartedly – you'll enjoy yourself all the more.

2 Smile
A smile goes a long way with local salespeople.

3 Don't Lose Your Head
Don't let your negotiations get too serious, and never raise your voice – it's taboo in Thailand.

4 Be Patient
Don't buy something from the first stall you visit. In Phuket, you'll almost always see it again.

5 Compare Prices
Get price quotes from different vendors selling the same goods; occasionally one vendor's prices are much lower than the others.

6 Buy In Bulk
Sellers often reduce their prices substantially if you buy more than one item.

7 Politely Ask For Discounts
The initial asking price is often about twice as high as the seller's final settling price.

8 Walk Away
The classic strategy is to politely say "No, thank you," and walk away. The vendor will often stop you and accept the price you offered.

9 Use Your Head
Avoid too-good-to-be-true prices, especially for expensive items such as gemstones or antiques.

10 Currency Exchange
Memorize your exchange rate so you can quickly calculate the cost in your home currency.

📖10 Phuket for Free

Celebrating the Vegetarian Festival

1 Festivals and Sporting Events

It seems there's always some sort of festival or sporting event taking place on the island (see pp74–5), and most of them are free, whether it's to watch and join in the goings on, or to cheer on the participants, such as at the Vegetarian Festival.

2 Bangla Road at Night

The main drag of Patong Beach comes alive in a blaze of neon and raucous music after dark (see p62). Since many of the bars are open-air, it's easy to soak up the buzz and people-watch in comfort.

3 Phromthep Cape Sunset

At the southernmost tip of the island, narrow Phromthep Cape (see p48) juts into the sea, and provides a spectacular view at sunset. There's a lighthouse on the cape with a small museum (free admission). The cape is popular

Macaque, Monkey Hill

with group tours, and those with their own transport can seek more isolated spots above Yanui Beach, a short distance north of the cape.

4 Wat Chalong

Phuket's largest and most popular temple (see pp16–17), located in the island's southeast, attracts both visitors and the Buddhist devout. Situated in the base of the Grand Pagoda, the murals depicting events in the life of the Buddha are a highlight.

5 Monkey Hill

Just to the east of Phuket town, Monkey Hill (see p13), also known as Khao To Sae, offers excellent viewpoints, a Taoist shrine, and a population of macaques. Feeding them is discouraged. Do watch your phone or camera carefully. They are great fun to watch, but afford them the respect you would any wild animal. The hill is also popular with fitness enthusiasts – the road is closed to vehicular traffic after 5pm, making it ideal for a sunset run. There's a small fitness park as well.

6 Karon Viewpoint

Located up in the hills south of Kata Beach, Karon Viewpoint (see p29) has superb views over both Kata beaches and Karon. Several shaded pavilions provide great spots for a picnic.

Sunset vistas from Karon Viewpoint

7 Buddhist Meditation Classes

MAP J4 ▪ 69/509 Soi Chaofah 5, Chalong ▪ 08727 97655 ▪ Classes: 11am Tue, 7pm Thu ▪ www.phuket-meditation.com

A free introductory lecture and class in the practice of Buddhist meditation is offered by the Phuket Meditation Center. Longer courses and retreats are also available.

8 Big Buddha

Clad in gleaming white marble, this 148-ft- (45-m-) tall statue *(see p82)* rests atop a hill near Wat Chalong and commands panoramic views of the island. It cost over 100 million Baht to construct, financed by donations from the faithful.

Lavish interiors of a Chinese shrine

9 Phuket Town Chinese Shrines

The faiths of Taoism, Mahayana Buddhism, and Confucianism have a vast pantheon of deities and spirits, to which these shrines *(see pp44–5)* pay homage. Visitors are welcome, but should remove shoes before entering and observe the decorum that these sacred places deserve.

10 Khao Rang Fitness Park

Located just north of Phuket Town, and famous for its viewpoints and good restaurants, Rang Hill *(see p13)* also offers a free outdoor fitness park with a variety of exercise devices such as inclined planes for sit-ups. The walk up to the park is a good warm-up.

Visitors at the street market

1 Bargaining is appropriate for any non-food item in a street market. Start with half the vendor's stated price and keep smiling.

2 Avoid using tuk-tuks as they are rarely a bargain, or get a price agreed on before using. Use Grab Taxi *(see p107)*, metered taxis, or rent a car or motor scooter.

3 The cheapest beach resort accommodation on the island is to be found in the Kata Beach hostels.

4 Eat in shopping-mall food courts. These are just above street stall price, but offer air-conditioned comfort.

5 Use budget airlines (Air Asia, Thai Smile) when flying in from Bangkok or elsewhere in the region.

6 Try Airbnb rentals for upscale accommodations at a much cheaper rate than the resorts.

7 Buy a local SIM card for your phone or tablet. These are available from shops selling phones as well as most convenience stores. Data speeds are good.

8 Imported alcoholic drinks are taxed up to 300 per cent here, but the local beers (Singha, Leo, Chang) are good, as is the rum – try Sang Som with soda and a squeeze of lime.

9 Traditional massage parlors don't offer the luxury found in upmarket spas, but these ubiquitous shops provide a good body or foot massage at a reasonable price.

10 Look for shops displaying a "VAT refund for tourists" sign, and claim the 7 per cent tax back on your purchases when you leave Thailand.

🔟 Festivals and Events

 Chinese New Year
Late Jan/early Feb

Celebrated with firecrackers, crashing cymbals, and colorful costumes, the Chinese New Year marks the beginning of a new lunar year, and is an auspicious day for the Chinese. The holiday is especially important in Phuket Town, where people dress in bright red costumes, and numerous parades and feasts are held.

Bang Neo Shrine at Chinese New Year

 Old Phuket Festival
Late Jan/early Feb

Chinese opera, rickshaw rides, and a Phuket Baba Light Show are a few of the highlights of this festival, which coincides with the Chinese New Year. The festival is held in Phuket Town on Thalang, Krabi, and Phuket roads.

3 Phuket Gay Pride Festival

Feb

Established in 1999, this festival seeks to create a stronger LGBTQ+ community in Phuket. For four nights each year, wild parties, parades, cabaret shows, fashion shows, and more take over Patong.

4 Phuket Food and Music Festival

Feb/Mar ▪ MAP B5 ▪ www.lagunaphuket.com

This popular festival is held at the Laguna complex of hotels and villas. Attracting a huge audience, it has a varied line up of musicians, with performances ranging from country music to jazz. Apart from the music, there are different food stalls and treats.

5 Songkran
Apr 13–15

The traditional Thai New Year celebration turns the entire country into one big water fight. Getting sprayed with water is considered good luck, and many Thais visit temples to pay respect to Buddha by sprinkling water on his statue.

6 Visakha Puja
May

Thailand's Buddhist temples overflow with merit-makers on this holy day marking the birth, enlightenment, and death of the Buddha – three events that occurred on the same day in different years. At night, believers walk around the temples in a candlelit procession.

Dazzling street parade marking the Phuket Gay Pride Festival

7 Por Tor Festival
Aug

During the annual "Hungry Ghosts" festival, offerings of special cakes, candles, and flowers are made to deceased ancestors, who are believed to revisit their earthly homes on this day. Chinese shrines serve as the center of the festival.

Lion dancer at the Por Tor Festival

8 Phuket Vegetarian Festival
Late Sep/early Oct ■ www.phuket vegetarian.com

This nine-day festival serves to "purify" participants and bring them good health, but has nothing to do with food. At Chinese shrines in Phuket Town, fire walking, and extreme acts of body piercing and self-mortification take place.

9 Loy Krathong
Late Oct/early Nov

Sins of the previous year float away as Thais pay homage to the guardian spirit of water. Small banana-leaf vessels are decorated with flowers and candles. If a person's boat floats, they will enjoy good luck for the year.

10 Patong Carnival
Nov

This three-day carnival combines, exhibitions, parades, live music, many street-side seafood stalls, and general revelry. The event also features displays telling the story of Patong's history.

TOP 10 SPORTING EVENTS

1 Muay Thai
No visit here is complete without witnessing this martial art form.

2 The Bay Regatta
Feb
More relaxed than the King's Cup, these races are popular with visitors.

3 Phuket Bike Week
Apr
This festival involves music, parties, and awesome motorbikes.

4 Phuket International Cricket Sixes Tournament
Apr
International cricketers come to Karon for this competition.

5 Phuket International Rugby Tournament
May
The three-day tournament draws teams from Australia and Asia.

6 Laguna Phuket International Marathon
Jun
The marathon starts at Bang Tao Beach.

7 Cape Panwa Hotel Phuket Race Week
Jul
A week of parties and yacht races, this festival attracts many participants.

8 Phuket Surfing Contest
Sep
At Kata Beach, this contest lets surfers vie for more than B100,000 in prizes.

9 Laguna Phuket Triathalon
Nov
A 1-mile (2-km) swim, 34-mile (55-km) cycle race, and 8-mile (13-km) run.

10 King's Cup Regatta
Dec
The King's Cup regatta began in 1987, to mark HM King Bhumibol's 60th birthday.

King's Cup Regatta on Kata Beach

TOP 10 Day Trips

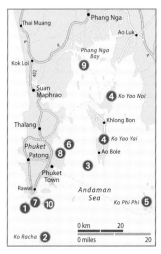

3 Ko Khai Nok
MAP F3

Another great snorkeling destination, this island has coral reefs hugging its coastline – the prime underwater attraction. Brilliantly colored parrot-fish can often be spotted. The small swimming cove features white sand flanked by rocky headlands. Vendors sell fresh coconut water from huts.

4 Ko Yao Yai and Ko Yao Noi
MAP F3

These picturesque islands in Phang Nga Bay feature charming thatched-roof homes and rubber plantations, interspersed with vast tracts of lush foliage. Most of the accommodations are on Ko Yao Noi, the smaller of the two islands. You can hire a kayak from your hotel to explore the beautiful rock formations facing the island. Alcohol is generally not sold here, except within hotel premises.

Beachfront at Ko Yao Yai Island

1 Ko Kaew
MAP H6

A Buddha statue greets visitors to this small island, which is visible from Phromthep Cape. A replica footprint of the Buddha makes this a holy pilgrimage site for some monks. On the island's far coast is another Buddhist shrine and *chedi* (stupa).

2 Ko Racha
MAP E4

Made up of two islands, Ko Racha is a renowned diving and snorkeling site. Ko Racha Yai has a few bunga-lows and restaurants, and a pretty beach. It's a great place for star-gazing. Smaller Ko Racha Noi is less developed, with rockier shorelines.

Ko Racha Yai beach

Breathtaking Ko Phi Phi Leh

5 Ko Phi Phi
MAP L4–M6

A speedboat from Rassada Port can whisk you to these islands in an hour, after which you can visit Viking Cave and beaches on Koh Phi Phi Leh, Monkey Beach, and some smaller islets nearby. The trip includes a stop for lunch on Ko Phi Phi Don. Catch an astonishing sunset from the stern on your way back to Phuket for dinner.

6 Ko Rang Yai
MAP L1

Home to the Phuket Pearl Farm, this private island cultivates three types of pearls for export. Ko Rang Yai also offers outdoor activities, including camping, mini-golf, and an air-gun shooting range. Visitors can watch demonstrations on how pearls are cultured, harvested, and turned into jewelry. The guides also explain how to tell the difference between real and fake pearls.

7 Ko Bon
MAP J6

A 15-minute boat ride from Rawai Beach, this small rocky island features a crescent-shaped beach

along the west coast. The beach has a quaint restaurant that serves seafood, Thai, and Western dishes. The island's east coast is owned by Evason Resorts and is for the exclusive use of their guests.

8 Ko Maphrao
MAP L2

With magnificent deserted beaches and coves, Ko Maphrao (its name means Coconut Island) is just five minutes by boat from Phuket's east coast. Popular activities here include swimming, snorkeling, and exploring the coastline's mangrove forests by boat. There's only one hotel, but the island also offers homestays with local families.

Ko Tapu limestone pillar

9 Ko Khao Phing Kan
Ever since *The Man with the Golden Gun* was filmed here, few people have referred to this island as Ko Khao Phing Kan. Now widely known as James Bond Island *(see p36)*, it is one of Phuket's most popular day trips. The famous limestone rock called Ko Tapu, or Nail Island, juts out of the sea nearby.

10 Ko Hae
MAP J6

Just 2 miles (3 km) off Phuket's southeastern shore, Ko Hae, or Coral Island, is a pretty island surrounded by colorful coral reefs. The island has two long sandy beaches – Long Beach and Banana Beach. The most popular activity here is exploring the vast Staghorn coral reefs, located around 328 ft (100 m) offshore.

Phuket
Area by Area

White-sand beach on Koh Miang in
the Similan Islands National Park

TOP 10 The South

Of the five million tourists who visit Phuket annually, the majority flock to Patong, Karon, and Kata on the island's southwest coast. Here, they find an array of world-class restaurants, activities, and hotels, all set amid the tropical backdrop of rolling green hills and crystal-blue waters. But most of southern Phuket, with its busy beaches, seaside restaurants, open-air bazaars, and throbbing nightclubs, doesn't aim to be an escape. Phuket Town, with its historical architecture, Chinese heritage, and southern Thai cuisine, is almost wholly distinct from Phuket's bustling tourist areas.

Statue at a Chinese shrine, Phuket Town

THE SOUTH

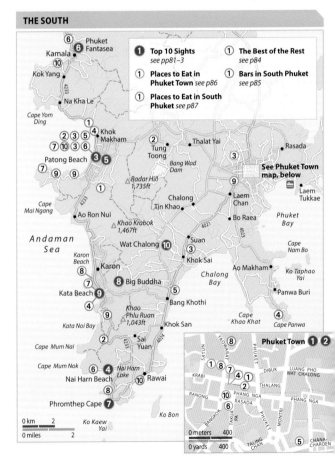

●	Top 10 Sights see pp81–3	①	The Best of the Rest see p84
①	Places to Eat in Phuket Town see p86	①	Bars in South Phuket see p85
①	Places to Eat in South Phuket see p87		

1 Phuket Vegetarian Festival

Dating back to the 1820s, the Phuket Vegetarian Festival *(see p13)* originated in Kathu after members of a Chinese opera contracted a fatal disease and sought ways to purify themselves and please the gods. During the nine-day event, participants practice acts of self-mortification, plunging spears through their cheeks, walking across burning-hot coals, and performing other gruesome displays of self-sacrifice.

2 Phuket Town

The capital of Phuket province, Phuket Town *(see pp12–15)* offers everything from world-class beaches and scenery to 100-year-old Straits Settlements mansions and shop houses (built when the island was one of Britain's Southeast Asian colonial territories). It also features traditional open-air markets and vividly hued Chinese shrines built during the tin boom of the late 19th and early 20th centuries. Walking tours are the best way to explore.

Tranquil Patong Beach

Historic street in Phuket Town

3 Patong Beach

This area *(see pp18–19)* is more relaxed these days, following the government clean-up campaign *(see p83)*. There are fewer hawkers, and motorized watercraft are only allowed in some areas, but there is a scarcity of sunbeds. The island's best dining can be found along the waterfront, with top restaurants commanding impressive views. The legendary nightlife in Patong needs little introduction. It runs the gamut from pulsating dance clubs to cabaret shows, open-air bars to adult venues ablaze in neon lights.

4 Nai Harn Beach

A picturesque bay on Phuket's far southwestern coast, Nai Harn *(see pp26–7)* remains one of the island's better-kept secrets. With just one beachfront resort, the landscape doesn't feel at all encroached upon. Tall screw pines populate the area behind the beach, providing a buffer between the nearby Buddhist monastery and Nai Harn Lake. Charming Nai Harn Town is a short motorbike or car ride from the beach, but is well worth a visit for its coffee shops and art studios.

5 Muay Thai

Two venues in Patong host regular bouts in which south Thai fighters pummel one another with elbows, shins, knees, and fists. Patong Boxing Stadium and Bangla Boxing Stadium *(see p18)* witness plenty of vicious knockouts. Foreign fighters come to train at the Muay Thai gyms here, and they often test their mettle in the rings. The music accompanying the fights is atmospheric – a haunting windpipe, tribal drums, and tiny finger cymbals.

Fireworks at Phuket Fantasea

6 Phuket Fantasea

MAP G1 ▪ 99 M3 Kamala Beach Kathu ▪ 07638 5000 ▪ Open 5–10pm Wed & Sat ▪ Adm ▪ www.phuket fantasea.fun

This lively theme park (see p60) is enough like Disneyland for kids to love it, and enough like Las Vegas for parents to enjoy it too. It is packed with fun activities, entertainment (see p62), and even shopping. The spectacular Fantasy of a Kingdom is the longest-running live show in Asia. Before this dazzling show, you can enjoy one of Asia's largest buffet dinners in the 4,000-seat dining facility at the Golden Kinnaree restaurant.

7 Phromthep Cape

On clear nights, a west-facing hilltop on Phuket's southern tip (see p27) feels like a large public gathering in anticipation of what could be a space shuttle launch or a fireworks show, with all eyes trained on the horizon. However, there is no such spectacle – the crowds are simply here to witness the sunset, and nature's show is indeed a spectacular one.

8 Big Buddha

MAP H4 ▪ Open 8am–6pm daily

This dramatic religious monument perched on top of Nakkerd Hill has become one of Phuket's iconic landmarks and attracts hundreds of visitors each day. The 148-ft- (45-m-) tall, cross-legged white marble Buddha makes an awesome sight when viewed from sea level, and offers even greater appeal from the hilltop, from where visitors can enjoy sweeping views and pleasant breezes. There's also the chance to enjoy a sunset dinner at Nakkerd Sea View Restaurant.

9 Kata Beach

Increasingly upscale, Kata (see pp28–9) draws positive reviews for the way in which it harmonizes its tropical beauty with ever-growing crowds and infrastructure. Indeed, the beach here offers many of the same joys as Patong, such as para-sailing and jet-skiing, yet it retains a decidedly more relaxed feel. At night, Kata has enough restaurants and

Phromthrep Cape's magnificent view

EXPLORING PHUKET'S SOUTHWEST COAST

nightlife to feel like it's got a pulse, but it isn't overbearing. With a wide selection of shopping, both on the beach and off, it's easy to see why Kata's popularity endures.

Shrine in Wat Chalong

⑩ Wat Chalong

The island's most famous Buddhist temple is located about 4 miles (6 km) south of Phuket Town. Wat Chalong (see pp16–17) features brilliantly colored buildings, including a glittering pagoda that was added to the complex in 2002. In 1876, during an uprising of migrant tin workers, the local Siamese fled here for protection. Two monks offered them shelter and helped resolve the dispute peacefully. Since then, the temple has been considered a place of pilgrimage. Today, many Thais visit the statues of Luang Pho Chaem and Luang Pho Chuang in the temple's sermon hall to seek their blessings.

⊙ MORNING

After hiring a car, start your journey in **Patong** (see p81), the tourist center of the island. Follow the road signs for Highway 4233 toward Karon, Kata, and Phromthep Cape. This coastal road takes you to the island's southern tip. Make your first stop at **Karon Beach** (see p51), one of Phuket's largest tourist beaches. Buy a coconut from a beach vendor and enjoy the fresh, sweet water inside. Continuing south on the road, you will pass the shop-lined streets of **Kata Beach**. Stop if something catches your eye. After Kata Noi, the road starts to ascend a steep hill that winds its way up to the famous **Karon Viewpoint** (see p84), from where you can enjoy breathtaking views and take fabulous photographs, so bring your camera. Continue to **Nai Harn Beach** (see p81), where a delicious seaside lunch awaits you under the shade of umbrellas and casuarina trees behind Nai Harn Beach.

AFTERNOON

After a relaxed lunch, follow the road signs to **Phromthep Cape**. You'll drive around **Nai Harn Lake** (see p27), and then up and down a hilly, tree-lined road. At the bottom of the hill is **Yanui Beach** (see p84), a charming place to swim, snorkel, and relax under the trees. The road then continues to Phromthep Cape, with its magnificent views over the Andaman Sea. Just be sure to reach Patong before it gets too dark. The journey takes about 45 minutes, and you don't want to be on these roads at night.

See map on p80

The Best of the Rest

 Soi Romanee
MAP N5

This old town street is a blast from the past with its restored guesthouses and cafés *(see p53)*. Look out for Jui Tui Chinese Temple *(see p45)*, the nexus of the Phuket Vegetarian Festival.

Jui Tui Chinese Temple

2 Karon Viewpoint
With great views of the island, this viewpoint is usually populated with vendors selling snacks and drinks, including fresh green coconut water *(see p29)*.

3 Chalong Bay Rum Distillery
MAP J4 ■ Soi Palai, Chaofah Road, Chalong ■ 093 575 1119 ■ Open 11am–6pm Mon–Sat (tours: 2–6pm, hourly)
The handcrafted white rum made here is distilled from sugar cane juice rather than molasses. The price of a tour includes a mojito.

4 Phuket Aquarium
MAP K5 ■ Sakdidet Road, Cape Panwa ■ 07639 1126 ■ Open 8:30am–4:30pm daily ■ Adm ■ www.phuket aquarium.org
This aquarium introduces visitors to the underwater world *(see p60)*.

 Chinese Shrines
The colorful shrines scattered throughout the island play an important role during the Phuket Vegetarian Festival *(see pp44–5)*.

6 Ao Sane Beach
This rugged, secluded little beach *(see p27)*, not far from Nai Harn, offers great opportunities for snorkeling and has a peaceful vibe.

 Paradise Beach
MAP G3 ■ Adm

Not far from the often crowded Patong Beach, this delightful little stretch emanates tranquility with its soft sand and palm trees; there is a coral reef not far off shore.

 Yanui Beach
This lovely cove *(see p26)* – an ideal setting for kayaking, snorkeling, or reading a book under the shade of palm trees – is located just past the windmill visible from Nai Harn Beach.

9 Emerald Beach
MAP G3

Thanks to its exposed location, this 1,640-ft- (500-m-) long beach, called Hat Tri Tra in Thai and tucked away south of Patong, offers a quiet place to hide out and work on your tan.

10 Rawai Beach
MAP H6

A non-swimming beach, Rawai is known for its seafood restaurants along the beach. Speedboats and long-tail boats can be chartered at Rawai to visit some of the smaller islands nearby.

Long-tail boats at Rawai Beach

Bars in South Phuket

 Patong Bay Hill
MAP H3 ▪ Soi Veerakit ▪ 07668 3060 ▪ www.patongbayhill.com
This resort *(see p64)* features several nightclubs and hosts many parties.

 Molly's Tavern
MAP N2 ▪ 94/1 Thaweewong Road, Patong ▪ 08691 16194 ▪ Open 9am–2am daily
This spirited Irish pub features live music every night.

 Roots Rock Reggae Bar
MAP P3 ▪ Nanai Road, Patong ▪ 087 271 4656 ▪ Open 1pm–2am daily
With regular barbeque and live music parties, this funky little reggae bar in Patong also features a small shop selling handmade jewelry, leather bags and belts, and more.

 Artspace Café and Music Bar
MAP H5 ▪ 7 Ket Kwan Road, Kata ▪ 090 156 0677 ▪ Open 3pm–4am daily
This bar has a cool bohemian vibe, with lots of plants and sculptures. It's a friendly place with a loyal following of visitors and locals. There's great food and live music every night.

 Kee Sky Lounge
MAP N2 ▪ 7th Floor, Kee Resort, Taweewong Road, Patong ▪ 08003 83374 ▪ Open 5:30–11pm
A fine place for sipping cocktails while enjoying the view of the sunset over Patong beach. Kee Sky Lounge has good food and great music to offer.

6 Café Del Mar
MAP G1 ▪ 118/18 Kamala, Kathu ▪ 09358 04486 ▪ Open noon–midnight daily ▪ www.phuket.cafedelmar.com
If you love electronic music, head to Café del Mar *(see p65)* and dance to sets from international DJs.

7 Kudo Beach Club
MAP N2 ▪ Patong Beach Road ▪ 076609401 ▪ Open 11am–midnight daily ▪ www.kudophuket.com
Enjoy Italian food, international DJs, and stiff cocktails at this beach club. It closes early compared to other bars.

8 Timber Hut
MAP P5 ▪ Yaowarat Road, Phuket Town ▪ 07621 1839 ▪ Open 7pm–2am daily
The house band here is considered one of the best on Phuket. There is a dance floor and seating upstairs.

Caribbean decor at After Beach Bar

9 After Beach Bar
MAP H5 ▪ Highway 4233 ▪ 08 474 59365 ▪ Open 9am–11pm daily
A wooden structure with a laid-back, Caribbean vibe, After Beach Bar is located near Karon Viewpoint and specializes in cocktails, seafood, and spectacular sunset views.

10 Illuzion Nightclub
MAP N2 ▪ Beach Road, Patong ▪ 07668 3030 ▪ Open 9pm–4am daily
One of Patong's best venues to dance the night away, Illuzion Nightclub *(see p64)* offers state of art music and light systems as well as great DJs.

See map on p80

Places to Eat in Phuket Town

1 Dibuk Restaurant
BB

Serving Thai and French cuisine, and offering a full selection of fine wines, this elegant restaurant *(see p14)* is set inside a traditional Straits Settlement house.

China Inn Café and Restaurant

2 China Inn Café and Restaurant
BB

The magnificent exterior of this shop house *(see p15)* gives way to a leafy courtyard, where diners can enjoy remarkable Thai and Western cuisine, and delightful Thai desserts.

3 Tunk-ka Cafe
MAP N4 ▪ Top of Rang Hill ▪ 07621 1500 ▪ Open 11am–10pm daily ▪ B

Atop Rang Hill, this outdoor café enjoys lovely views and a reputation for the best iced coffee on Phuket.

4 Kopitiam by Wilai
MAP P5 ▪ 18 Thalang Road, Phuket Town ▪ 083 606 9776 ▪ Open 11am–9pm Mon (to 8pm Tue, Thu & Fri, to 6pm Sun) ▪ B

With an old-fashioned feel and photographs of Phuket in bygone eras, Kopitiam is owned by the same family that runs Wilai next door.

5 Laemthong Seafood
MAP Q6 ▪ Chana Charoen Road ▪ 089 549 4992 ▪ Open 11am–10pm daily ▪ B

The oldest Chinese restaurant on Phuket is popular for its seafood and Chinese cuisine, including oyster omelets, and Peking chicken.

6 Ka Jok See
MAP P5 ▪ 26 Takua Pa Road, near Rasada Circle ▪ 095 032 7112 ▪ Open 6pm–midnight Tue–Sat ▪ B

Served in a charming old shop house, the fixed-price dinner is followed by dancing and a cabaret show *(see p62)*. It's a full-evening experience for which reservations are required.

7 Wilai Restaurant
MAP P5 ▪ 14 Thalang Road ▪ Open 7am–2pm daily ▪ B

A selection of pre-cooked curries and stir-fries is served at this popular spot. *Penang Moo* (coconut milk curry with pork) is highly rated.

8 Ran Jee Nguat
MAP P5 ▪ Corner of Yaowarat and Dibuk roads ▪ Open 10am–8pm daily ▪ B

This Chinese-run restaurant serves one of the island's best-loved local specialties – *kanom chine naam ya phuket* (Chinese noodles in a puréed fish and curry sauce).

9 Roti Chao Fa
MAP N5 ▪ Chao Fa Road ▪ Open 6am–noon daily ▪ B

Delicious curries served with flat bread and teas make this a popular choice for breakfast.

10 Anna's Café
MAP P5 ▪ Rasada Road ▪ 062 068 1999 ▪ Open 11am–10pm daily ▪ BB

This restaurant serves upscale Thai food family-style. The *massaman* (beef curry) and *gaeng som* (sour curry) are two favorite dishes here.

Places to Eat in South Phuket

① White Box Restaurant
MAP H2 ▪ 247/5 Prabaramee Road, Kalim Beach ▪ 07634 6271 ▪ Open 5pm–1am daily ▪ BBB

The restaurant *(see p66)* features both Thai and international dishes with a setting adjacent to the Andaman Sea.

② Thong Dee Brasserie
MAP J2 ▪ Soi Bangthong 110/25, Kathu ▪ 07631 9323 ▪ Open 4–10pm Tue–Sun ▪ BB

A reasonably priced restaurant *(see p66)* offering Thai and international cuisine. The Thai delicacies are from different regions of the country. Try the *kaeng pod* (spicy red curry).

③ Il Pomodoro
MAP N1 ▪ 186, 14 Thawewong Road, Patong ▪ 090 912 2851 ▪ Open 2–11pm daily ▪ BB

Feast on wood-fired pizzas and traditional pastas (including good gluten-free and vegan options) on Patong Beach.

Breathtaking views from Baan Rim Pa

④ Baan Rim Pa
MAP H2 ▪ 223 Prabaramee Road, Kalim Beach ▪ 07634 0879 ▪ Open 1–11pm daily ▪ BBB

Enjoy royal Thai cuisine and soak in the views of Kalim Bay here *(see p67)*.

⑤ Kan Eang
MAP J4 ▪ 9/3 Chofa Road, Chalong Bay ▪ 083 173 1187 ▪ Open 10am–11pm daily ▪ BB

On Phuket's eastern coast, Kan Eang serves classic Chinese-Thai seafood.

⑥ Sala Bua
MAP N1 ▪ 41 Thaweewongse Road, 83150 Patong ▪ 07634 0138 ▪ Open 6am–midnight daily ▪ BBB

Imaginative East-West fusion dishes, with a focus on seafood, served up at a spacious and breezy beachfront location *(see p67)*.

⑦ The Boathouse Restaurant
MAP H5 ▪ 182, Koktanode Road, Kata Beach ▪ 07633 0015 ▪ Open 6:30am–11pm daily ▪ BBB

Known for its wine list, this beachfront restaurant *(see p66)* serves French and Thai dégustation menus.

⑧ On the Rock
MAP H4 ▪ 47 Karon Road, Marina Phuket, Karon Beach ▪ 07633 0625 ▪ Open noon–10pm daily ▪ BBB

This beachside restaurant *(see p66)*, specializing in Thai and international seafood, is open for lunch, as well as dinner.

⑨ La Gritta
MAP N1 ▪ Amari Coral Beach Resort, Patong Beach ▪ 07634 0106 ▪ Open 11am–midnight daily ▪ BB

In a quiet bayside setting, this Italian restaurant specializes in gourmet pizzas and handmade pastas.

⑩ Silk
MAP G1 ▪ Andara Resort & Villas, Kamala Beach ▪ 07633 8777 ▪ Open 7am–10pm daily ▪ BBB

This restaurant *(see p66)* is part of the Andara Resort, offering international cuisine coupled with a stunning view of the sea from Kamala Beach.

See map on p80

TOP 10 The North

Virgin rain forest, mangroves, wildlife sanctuaries, and unspoiled golden-sand beaches where giant leatherback turtles return each year to lay their eggs – northern Phuket abounds in opportunities to connect with the area's magnificent natural surroundings. Jungle trekking trails, a half-buried golden Buddha statue, and picturesque swimming coves comprise natural and historic wonders, while theme parks, golf courses, and tree-top canopies also attract many visitors. The beaches north of Kamala offer more privacy, tranquility, and access to nature for those who seek a little more space – and less bustle – during their holiday on Phuket.

Wat Prathong

THE NORTH

Tha Chat Chai
Tha Taling Chan
Dan Yit
To Nong Bay
Laem Phrao
Ba Kan
Suan Maphrao
Ao Tu Khun
Mai Khao Beach
Khao Ban Bang Duk 875ft
Andaman Sea
Mai Khao
Mak Prok
Phuket ✈
Laem Sai
Sirinat National Park
Blue Canyon Country Club
Ban Chathu
Laem Khat
Muang Mai
Ban Phara
Cape Sai Khru
Sakoo
Ao Kung
Ban Paw
Khao Sai Khru 1,100ft
Bang Khanun
Ko Raet
Nai Thon
Khao Phra Thaeo Royal Forest and Wildlife Reserve
Gibbon Rehabilitation Project
Na Sok
Bang Pae
Wat Prathong
Nok Le
Pa Khlok
Ko Tha
Thalang
Bang Rong Bay
Bang Tao Bay
Li Phuan
Phak Chit
Ao Yabu
Cape Son
Cherngtalay
Liphon Hua Han
Cape Yamu
Bang Tao
Ma Nik
Tha Rua
Thalang National Museum
Surin Plaza
Laem Singh Beach
Phuket Boat Lagoon

1 Top 10 Sights
see pp91–3

1 Places to Eat
see p97

1 Places to Shop
see p96

1 The Best of the Rest
see p94

1 Outdoor Activities
see p95

0 km   2
0 miles   2

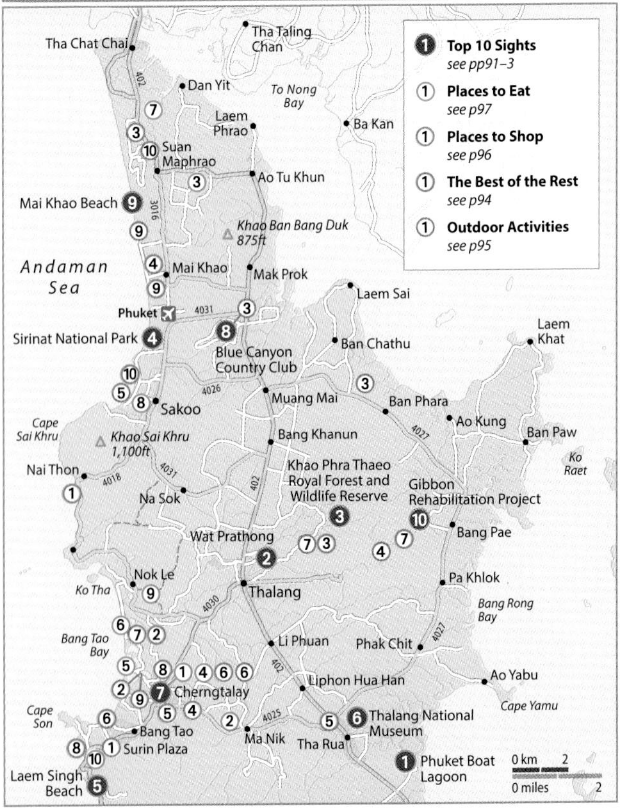

Previous pages Aerial view of the iconic Big Buddha statue atop Nakkerd Hill

Rows of yachts moored at the Phuket Boat Lagoon

① Phuket Boat Lagoon
MAP K1 ■ 22/1 Moo 2
Thepkasattri Road ■ 07623 9055
■ www.phuketboatlagoon.com

Luxury yachts from around the world are moored in the lagoon and up-scale marina here. Opened in 1994, the Phuket Boat Lagoon features more than 150 units with restaurants, retail outlets, and sport complexes. The Boat Lagoon Resort has 300 guest rooms, exceptional restaurants, tennis courts, swimming pools, and a Thai spa.

② Wat Prathong
MAP C5 ■ Highway 402
■ Open 8am–5:30pm daily

The half-buried golden Buddha image here draws worshippers and curious tourists alike. Built in the 1750s, Wat Prathong has received many high-profile visitors, including King Rama V in 1909. The statue was most likely half buried as a result of flooding. The reclining gilded Buddha is another popular attraction. The colorful temple complex also features a museum that houses assorted historical items, such as tin-mining tools and Javanese daggers.

③ Khao Phra Thaeo Royal Forest and Wildlife Reserve
Home to numerous protected animal species, as well as rare plant life, this virgin rain forest has a number of jungle trekking trails, two lovely waterfalls, and a gibbon rehabilitation facility. Declared a wildlife sanctuary in 1969, Khao Phra Thaeo (see pp20–21) contains an especially rare palm species, found only here and called the white-backed palm, which was only identified in 1929. Animals include barking deer, gibbons, and flying foxes, as well as snakes and wild pigs.

④ Sirinat National Park
The pristine shoreline along Phuket's northwestern coast is protected by Thailand's national park service. Every winter, massive sea turtles lay their eggs in the sand here, while virgin mangrove forests can be found at the northern end of the park. A 2,625-ft- (800-m-) long wooden walkway has been built over the mangroves and is a popular scenic walk. The Sirinat National Park (see pp22–3) protects the pristine Mai Khao, Nai Yang, and Nai Thon beaches, which are a world apart from the raucous party beaches.

The serene Nai Yang Beach

5 Laem Singh Beach
MAP G1

This beautiful, hidden beach (see p51), populated by lush palm trees and giant rocks, feels like a secret cove. However, despite being accessible only by boat from the nearby Surin beach (see p50), this beach remains a popular destination throughout the year and becomes especially busy during high season. The rocky areas in the water provide excellent snorkeling opportunities, while the rustic wooden beach restaurants offer tree-shaded spots in which to enjoy fresh seafood.

Palm-fringed Bang Tao Beach

6 Thalang National Museum
MAP D6 ■ Thalang ■ 07631 1025 ■ Open 9am–4pm Wed–Sun ■ Adm

In 1785, two Siamese women helped defend Phuket against an attack by Burmese soldiers (see pp40–41). This museum (see p46), and the Heroines' Monument (see p43) were built in the honor of their bravery. A large 9th-century statue of Vishnu, the Hindu god, stands in the museum's main hallway, while other displays feature the island's tin-mining history, its Moken communities, and more.

SEA TURTLES

During the November to February breeding season, giant sea turtles, including the magnificent leatherback, return to the northwestern beaches of Phuket – to the same place they were born – to lay their eggs. Mai Khao and Nai Yang beaches provide perfect nesting sites where sea turtles can lay their eggs and bury them in the sand for protection until they hatch.

7 Horseback Rides on Bang Tao Beach
MAP B6 ■ Open 9am–5:30pm daily ■ Adm

Visitors can ride horses from the Phuket Laguna Riding Club on the beautiful golden sands of Phuket's second-longest beach. The experience provides marvelous photo opportunities, as well as being adventurous, as the horses walk, trot, or canter through the calm waters and past stunning scenery. Everyone is catered for – from regular riders to novices, who are well looked after by experienced guides – and all equipment is provided.

8 Blue Canyon Country Club
MAP C3 ■ 165, Moo 1 Thepkasattri Road, Thalang ■ 07632 8088 ■ www. bluecanyonphuket.com

Golf aficionados rave about Blue Canyon's rolling fairways, towering trees, and exceptionally well-kept greens. The two picturesque championship courses here, the Canyon and the Lakes, are premier golfing destinations. The Canyon Course has hosted the Johnnie Walker Classic three times, playing host to a number of acclaimed golfers. The 17th hole on the Canyon Course is considered one of the 500 best in the world, according to *Golf Magazine*. Non-golfers will enjoy the club's spa and fine dining facilities.

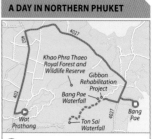

Khao Phra Thaeo Royal Forest and Wildlife Reserve

Gibbon Rehabilitation Project

Bang Pae Waterfall

Wat Prathong

Ton Sai Waterfall

Bang Pae

MORNING

Hire a private car for this itinerary if you don't have a rented one, since the journey covers quite a bit of ground. Also carry sturdy shoes, swimwear, and a towel. Start the day auspiciously by making merit at **Wat Prathong** *(see p91)*, where local Buddhists revere the half-buried golden Buddha image. The temple is located quite far inland, so it isn't as crowded as Wat Chalong. Continue eastward to the nearby **Khao Phra Thaeo Royal Forest and Wildlife Reserve** *(see p91)*, one of the last remaining habitats for native animals on Phuket. Here, park your car near **Bang Pae Waterfall** *(see p94)* and eat at one of the restaurants near the car park. Better still, buy a take-away meal and enjoy a picnic in the shade near the waterfall.

AFTERNOON

A short walk from the Bang Pae Waterfall stands the small **Gibbon Rehabilitation Project**, where gibbons who have been ill-treated in captivity are gently reintroduced into a wild habitat. After watching these fascinating creatures from the viewing platform, you can adopt a baby gibbon for a small amount of money and ensure that the animal continues to receive vital care. If you're feeling energetic, hike the 5-mile- (8-km-) long jungle path to **Ton Sai Waterfall** *(see p94)*. When it's time for a bite to eat, visit the floating restaurant located in the coastal mangrove swamps, which are also a protected area. Return to your hotel by the early evening.

 Mai Khao Beach

Part of Sirinat National Park, this 6-mile- (10-km-) long beach *(see p23)* has undulating golden sand lined by palm trees and pines. Development in the area has been limited, resulting in resorts that truly respect the surroundings. The sea can be rough in summer, but the beach makes for an excellent scenic trek, and walkers often find themselves alone with the birds.

Gibbon Rehabilitation Project

Established in 1992, this center *(see pp20–21)* seeks to rehabilitate captive white-handed gibbons and reintroduce them into their natural habitat, while striving to end their illegal use as tourist attractions and pets. You can pay a small donation to adopt a gibbon that has been mistreated in captivity.

Gibbons at the Rehabilitation Project

See map on p90

The Best of the Rest

1 Nai Thon Beach
MAP A4

A sleepy little hideaway, this beach is usually free of large tourist crowds. The reefs are popular with divers.

2 Laguna Phuket Golf Club
MAP B6 ■ 34 Moo 4, Srisoonthorn Road, Cherngtalay ■ 07632 4350 ■ www.lagunaphuket golf.com

Voted one of the best resorts in Asia, this golf club features scenic lagoons and immaculate greens.

3 Cable Jungle Adventure Phuket
MAP C5 ■ 232/17 Bansuaneramit, Moo 8, Srisoonthorn Road ■ 081977 4904 ■ Open 9am–6pm daily ■ www.cablejunglephuket.com

With 15 stations and a 3,937-ft- (1,200-m-) long zipline run, this is a great treetop canopy adventure.

4 Wat Mai Khao
MAP B3

A serene and unadorned temple in a quiet forested area near Mai Khao village, Wat Mai Khao also has a bird sanctuary within its compound.

5 Heroines' Monument
MAP C6 ■ Thepkasattri Road, north of Phuket Town

This monument (see p47) is a tribute to the sisters who helped defend Phuket from invaders in the 18th century.

6 Windsurfing in Bang Tao
MAP B6

Bang Tao enjoys the reputation of being one of Phuket's best places to windsurf. Boards and sails can be rented from local resorts and shops.

7 Surin Beach
MAP A6

This beach houses some of Phuket's top-end resorts such as The Chedi. The area's wealth is reflected in the neighboring homes and restaurants.

8 Bang Pae and Ton Sai Waterfalls

The two waterfalls in Khao Phra Thaeo Royal Forest and Wildlife Reserve, linked by a hiking trail, are picturesque destinations surrounded by beautiful jungle scenery (see p20).

Water gushing at Bang Pae waterfall

9 Splash Jungle Waterpark
MAP B3 ■ 65/179 Moo 4, Mai Khao Soi 4, Mai Khao Beach ■ 07637 2111 ■ Open 10am–5:45pm daily ■ Adm ■ www.splashjungle.com

With thrilling rides, this theme park is an ideal place to splash around.

10 Nai Yang Beach
MAP B4

A popular picnic destination for locals, this tree-lined beach has restaurants that serve a selection of delicious seafood.

Sailing boats on Bang Tao Beach

Outdoor Activities

Snorkelers enjoying Phuket's crystal-clear waters

 Snorkeling
There are many opportunities to see beautiful underwater coral formations and colorful schools of fish in and around Phuket. In winter, the clear waters off Surin, Nai Yang, and Nai Thon make for great dives.

 Canoeing
Go canoeing in the incredible mangrove forests and sea caves along Phuket's northeastern and northwestern coasts.

3 Golfing
MAP B6
Some of Phuket's best golf courses can be found in the north. Mission Hills, Blue Canyon, and Laguna Phuket offer picturesque, challenging, and well-maintained courses.

4 Trekking
Northern Phuket's most scenic trek covers 4 miles (6 km) of jungle trails in the Khao Phra Thaeo Royal Forest and Wildlife Reserve. Guides can be hired at the visitor center near Bang Pae Waterfall (see p94).

5 Kite Surfing
With good year-round winds, Phuket's west coast is ideal for kite-surfing enthusiasts. Nai Yang Beach, which is free of speedboats and jet-skis, has a great kite school that offers classes for beginners. From December to March, the school is based at Chalong Bay (see p56).

 Horseback Riding
The Phuket Laguna Riding Club and Phuket Riding Club offer horseback rides along the seashore at Bang Tao Beach (see p92).

 Ziplining
Soar through the jungle canopy safely harnessed and clipped to a cable that runs from one station to the next. It's an adrenaline rush, but take the time to focus on the beauty of the surroundings as well (see p21).

8 Cycling
A bicycle tour is a great way to experience northern Phuket's back roads and trails. Popular trips involve cruising through stunning scenery past villages and plantations in the island's northeast. Cycling trips can last either half a day, a full day, or overnight (see p55).

 Camping
MAP B3
Visitors can pitch a tent on parts of Nai Yang and Mai Khao beaches in the Sirinat National Park. The park's visitor center, at the southern end of Mai Khao, rents out camping gear.

10 Swimming
Excellent swimming beaches stretch from Kamala to Mai Khao, on Phuket's northwestern coast. Be cautious during the rainy season, however, as undertows and currents can be strong. Look out for red flags.

See map on p90

Places to Shop

1 The Plaza Surin
MAP A6 ▪ 07627 1241
▪ **Open 9am–7pm daily**
Close to Surin beach, this mall offers everything from high end art objects to clothing in its dozen distinct boutiques.

2 The Courtyard Phuket
MAP B6 ▪ Canal Village, Laguna Phuket Resort, Bang Tao ▪ 076 264 4689 ▪ Open 9am–6pm daily ▪ www.jimthompson.com
The famed silk retail shop Jim Thompson has a good outlet in this shopping center. You can also find leather goods and ceramics here.

3 Mai Khao Plaza
MAP B2 ▪ Near Marriott Resort ▪ 07636 2330 ▪ Open 10am–11pm daily
This place features a good mixture of boutiques, travel-necessity shops, hair salon, massage parlor, and mid-range restaurants.

4 Lemongrass House
MAP B5 ▪ 10/2 M.1, T. Cherngtalay, A.Thalang ▪ 07632 5501 ▪ Open 9am–6pm daily ▪ www.lemongrasshousethailand.com
With some 90 aromas to choose from, the spa products sold here are among the best in Asia. Customers can even blend their own products.

5 Talat Nat Local Markets
MAP C5 ▪ Talat Nat: opposite the Cherng Talay Police Station; open 1–8pm Wed & Sun
A *talat nat* market offers inexpensive clothing, snacks, and handicrafts. A *talat sot* market offers fresh food, fruits, and vegetables. Venues and times vary.

6 Heritage Collection
MAP B6 ▪ 106/19–20 Bang Tao Beach Road, Cherngtalay ▪ 07632 5818 ▪ Open 9am–9pm daily
Find antique wood and bronze Buddha images from southeast Asia along with Chinese sculptures, imperial clothing, and furniture here.

7 Banyan Tree Gallery
MAP B6 ▪ Laguna Phuket Resort, Bang Tao ▪ 07637 2400 ▪ www.banyantreegallery.com
Showcasing Indigenous handicrafts (home furnishings, apparel, candles, jewelry) by artisans from around the world, this gallery seeks to conserve traditional crafts and skills.

Handicrafts at Banyan Tree Gallery

8 Boat Avenue Street Mall
MAP C5 ▪ Thepkrasattri Road ▪ 07630 4635
Thailand's best source of imported foods, Villa Market can be found here. Find good handicrafts at the Friday evening weekend market.

9 Canal Village
MAP B6 ▪ Laguna Phuket Resort, Bang Tao ▪ www.lagunaphuket.com/canalvillage
An outdoor mall offering clothing, jewelry, sports equipment, and local products, plus restaurants and cafés.

10 Turtle Village Shopping Centre
MAP B2 ▪ Open 9am–10pm daily
This upscale shopping center in Mai Khao offers unique Thai souvenirs as well as silk, artwork, and more.

Places to Eat

 Mrs. B
MAP B6 ■ 19/1 Lagoon Road, Cherngtalay ■ 093 586 9828 ■ BB
Enjoy Australian meats and local seafood, grilled over a wood fire, at this buzzing restaurant and bar.

 Suay
MAP B6 ■ 177/99 Moo 6 Si Sunthon, Cherngtalay ■ 09333 91890 ■ BBB
Take a seat in the gorgeous garden and tuck into delicious Thai and European dishes. The seafood is particularly good.

Jakkajan Seafood Restaurant
MAP B2 ■ Soi 5 Mae Khao 6 ■ 08189 13731 ■ B
Fresh seafood is served up in a casual, Thai-style environment at Jakkajan.

 Tatonka Restaurant
MAP B6 ■ 382/19 Moo 1, 34 Lagoon Road Cherngtalay ■ 07632 4349 ■ BB
Influenced by Mediterranean, Asian, and Latin American cuisines, the fusion fare is commendable. Try the sashimi spring rolls and Peking duck pizza.

La Trattoria
MAP B6 ■ Dusit Thani Laguna ■ 390 Moo1, Srisoontorn Road, Cherngtalay ■ 07636 2999 ■ BBB
Located in an elegant resort, this retaurant specializes in Italian cuisine, and has good options for vegetarians. The locally caught sea bass and tiger prawns are a must-try.

Paul
MAP B6 ■ Bang Tao Beach, Cherngtalay ■ 083 5019429 ■ BB
Overlooking the beach, this restaurant serves simple and tasly Thai dishes. It's the perfect choice for a sunset dinner.

PRICE CATEGORIES
For a three-course meal for two with half a bottle of wine (or equivalent meal), taxes, and extra charges.
....
B under B500 **BB** B500–1,000
BBB over B1,000

 Kin Dee Restaurant
MAP B2 ■ 71/6 Moo 5, Mai Khao Beach ■ 07632 8293 ■ BB
Try the crabmeat stir fried with curry powder at this seafood restaurant.

Black Ginger
MAP B6 ■ Slate Resort Nai Yang Beach ■ 07632 7006 ■ BBB
Situated in a Thai style pavilion on a lake within the upscale Slate Resort, this place has a lovely ambience and serves superb Thai cuisine.

360° Restaurant
MAP B6 ■ The Pavilions Phuket, 31/1 Moo 6, Cherngtalay ■ 07631 7600 ■ BBB
On a hilltop at The Pavilions Phuket, this romantic restaurant is known for its tuna tartar, smoked pork back ribs, and dark chocolate fondue.

360° Restaurant at twilight

 Blue Lagoon
MAP A6 ■ Srisoontorn Road ■ 087 923 8235 ■ B
This family-run, beachfront restaurant is decorated with almospheric lantern lights. The menu features classic Thai dishes. It has vegetarian options, too.

See map on p90

TOP 10 Farther Afield

Try to imagine the perfect tropical landscape, and you will probably conjure up almost exactly the scenery that surrounds Phuket – unspoiled white-sand beaches, enchanting underwater worlds, ancient rain forests, and dramatic limestone cliffs. There are also hundreds of bird species, rare plants and flowers, native animals, colorful coral reefs, and awe-inspiring vistas. Easily accessible from Phuket as day trips, southern Thailand's natural wonders draw millions of visitors each year, but at their farthest reaches – when trekking on jungle trails, immersed in the azure sea, kayaking in cave grottoes, or boating through sparsely populated bays – you'll often find yourself alone.

Junk in Phang Nga Bay

FARTHER AFIELD

Top 10 Sights
see pp99–101

Places to Eat on Ko Phi Phi
see p103

The Best of the Rest
see p102

Tonsai Village

Similan Islands coral reef

1 Similan Islands

One of the world's premier scuba diving destinations, the Similan Islands *(see pp30–31)* offer underwater landscapes renowned for their staggering colors and marine life. The most popular dive sites include East of Eden, Richelieu Rock, and Anita's Reef, where colorful seascapes abound. Located in the Andaman Sea, about 31 miles (50 km) from Khao Lak, the Similans are best visited as part of an overnight or multiday tour. Non-divers can enjoy snorkeling, boat tours, and visits to uninhabited islands.

2 Khao Sok National Park

Home to native wildlife, such as the Malaysian tapir, wild boars, and pig-tailed macaque monkeys, this national park is one of Thailand's most pristine virgin rain forests. The majestic scenery features deep valleys, towering limestone cliffs, lakes, and jungle paths. Adventures into the park often include elephant treks, canoeing, and jeep safaris. Picturesque Cheow Laan Lake *(see pp32–5)*, framed by verdant cliffs, is home to floating bamboo-raft houses, and the area is a favorite with photographers and bird-watchers.

3 Natai Beach
MAP E2

On the mainland just north of Phuket Island, Natai is perfect for anyone seeking an easily accessible hideaway. A 20-minute drive from the airport (closer than some beach areas), it is totally devoid of jet-skis, speedboats, or beach-bed vendors. Accommodation is mainly upscale, although there are also budget options, too. This is Phuket as it was in years long gone by.

4 Phi Phi Viewpoint
MAP M5

Enjoy breathtaking views of the sunrise from Ko Phi Phi Don's highest point *(see p101)*, some 610 ft (186 m) above sea level. With first light, the island's dumbbell shape can be seen beyond the treetops, as well as the dramatic rock formations on the far side of the island. The trip to the summit doesn't take much time or effort – it's just 20 minutes or so from Loh Dalum Bay.

Limestone pillars in Cheow Laan Lake, Khao Sok National Park

The cliffed Phang Nga Bay

5 Phang Nga Bay

Dramatic limestone cliffs jut up from this bay (see pp36–7), providing extraordinary scenery for boat cruises, kayak journeys, and island tours. To experience the bay fully, spend an entire day here, venturing beyond the popular tourist sites such as Ko Phing Kan and Ko Panyee. Kayak tours explore cave tunnels that open into fantastic *hongs* (lagoons). Traditional junk boats, long-tail boats, and speed-boats can be hired along Phuket's east coast piers, as well as from Chalong and Rawai Beach.

ECO CONTROVERSY

Ko Phi Phi Leh's Maya Bay, which after being the filming location of *The Beach* became popular with tourists, had to be closed indefinitely in 2018 owing to environmental concerns. The decision was taken to protect the fragile coral life. However, the status should be confirmed locally.

6 Ko Phi Phi Leh
MAP F3

Framed on three sides by steep limestone cliffs, and caressed by calm crystal blue waters, also has Koh Pida Islets, just off the southern tip. The two tiny islets have steep cliffs that plunge into the sea. With its richly diverse marine life, the area offers some of the best snorkeling and scuba diving experiences.

7 Khao Lak
MAP E2

Pristine jungles hug the coastline, while the clear waters and white-sand beaches of Khao Lak offer a natural paradise for those seeking tranquillity. A number of fascinating diving and snorkeling sites, hidden beaches, and upscale resorts populate Khao Lak. The Khao Sok Lam Ru National Park features beautiful sea cliffs, estuaries, and mangroves. Treks and long-tail boat trips can be arranged at the park's visitor center. The 2004 tsunami devastated Khao Lak, but the area has made a strong recovery, and today tourism is flourishing again.

8 Ko Panyee
MAP F2

Most of this small island consists of a massive limestone outcrop that rises vertically out of Phang Nga Bay. The main attraction here is the stilt village constructed in the shallow waters along the island's south side. The island's economy today relies increasingly on day-trippers from nearby Phuket. Fresh seafood restaurants line the shore, and a mosque towers over the village. Visitors often visit Ko Panyee and Ko Phing Kan combined as part of a packaged tour.

9 Ko Phi Phi Don
MAP M5

Once populated by fishermen, and later home to vast coconut plantations, this beautiful island southeast of Phuket is now a thriving tourist destination. With colorful bays framed by cliffs and turquoise waters, Ko Phi Phi Don possesses physical beauty but also has a thriving nightlife and many convenience stores. Although the 2004 tsunami destroyed much of Ko Phi Phi Don, it has now been almost entirely rebuilt.

Ko Phi Phi Don's main street

10 King Cruiser Wreck Dive
MAP F3

On May 4, 1997, a ferry on a trip from Phuket to Ko Phi Phi collided with a reef pinnacle and sank. The crew and passengers were all rescued. Today the sunken cruiser remains a popular and relatively uncomplicated dive site, reachable with standard scuba gear. The ship features large openings that offer easy access to the boat's interior *(see p36)*.

Rugged Ko Panyee island

DAY TRIP TO KO PHI PHI

Monkey Beach
Rassada Port 25 miles (40 km)
Ko Phi Phi Don
Loh Dalum Beach
Tonsai Beach
Viking Cave
Ko Phi Phi Leh

▶ **MORNING**

Set your alarm clock for early in the morning, and catch the boat that leaves **Rassada Port** *(see pp106–7)* on Phuket's east coast at 8:30am. Choose a tour company that arranges pickups from your hotel. Onboard the passenger ferry to Ko Phi Phi, breakfast on coffee, sandwiches, and fresh fruit on the open-air roof deck or in an air-conditioned cabin. After dropping off some travelers at **Ko Phi Phi Don**, the boat continues to the nearby **Ko Phi Phi Leh** where you can visit a superb beach, Pileh Lagoon. You can go snorkeling here before visiting other beautiful bays. Some beaches are accessible only after a short trek, which adds to the fun. Visit **Viking Cave** *(see p102)*, which is famed for its ancient carvings depicting historic scenes. For lunch, the boat returns to Ko Phi Phi Don, where a decadent buffet awaits.

AFTERNOON

After lunch, relax on the famous twin bays of **Tonsai Beach** and **Loh Dalum**. These beaches have sun beds with umbrellas, while the comfortably warm blue waters remain shallow even quite a long way from the shore. You can also visit **Monkey Beach** *(see p102)*, home to many of these curious creatures. It also offers good snorkeling and opportunities to see colorful fish and coral. Dine at your hotel – to get back in time, take the ferry on its return to Phuket around 4:45pm.

See map on p98 ←

The Best of the Rest

 Ko Yao Noi
MAP F3

Popular for its eco-friendly homestay programs, Ko Yao Noi remains an idyllic and rustic destination in Phang Nga Bay. Visitors appreciate its quiet beaches, slow-paced lifestyle, picturesque hiking trails, and kayaking.

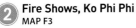 **Fire Shows, Ko Phi Phi**
MAP F3

Flaming staffs and twirling fiery orbs create a tribal feel during the nightly fire shows on the beach on Ko Phi Phi Don.

Fire show performer, Ko Phi Phi

 Ko Hae (Coral Island)
MAP J6

Nicknamed for the impressive coral reef surrounding the island, this day-trip destination off Phuket's east coast has two pristine beaches.

4 **Surin Islands National Marine Park**
MAP E2

Most easily accessed from Khao Lak, this chain of islands spans nearly 58 sq miles (150 sq km) of underwater area. Pristine under water reefs make this a popular destination for divers.

5 **Viking Cave**
MAP F4

This cave, at Ko Phi Phi Leh, has ancient carvings resembling Viking-style vessels. These petroglyphs confirm the legends of Viking boats visiting the Andaman coast.

 Camping on the Beach at Ko Similan
MAP D2

The tent campgrounds on Ko Similan allow visitors to spend a night on the beach, listening to the waves and watching the sky ablaze with stars.

7 **Ko Jum and Ko Si Boya**
MAP F3

This adjacent pair of secluded islands, featuring great beaches, sea caves, and snorkeling, is reached from the Ko Phi Phi islands by speedboat in an hour. Once home only to the Moken, they have very little tourist infrastructure beyond guesthouses – and therein lies the attraction.

8 **Loh Dalum Beach**
MAP M6

This splendid tropical beach on Ko Phi Phi Don features limestone cliffs encircling a white-sand beach.

9 **Nightlife on Ko Phi Phi**
MAP F3

Many people visit Ko Phi Phi for the natural beauty of the islands. Another major draw is Ko Phi Phi Don's legendary nightlife, which includes everything from cocktail buckets and beach bars to fire dancing.

10 **Monkey Beach**
MAP L5

While some come to Ko Phi Phi Don to take photographs of the pesky monkeys on the beach, others come for the snorkeling opportunities at the fabulous reef located offshore.

Monkeys on the beach

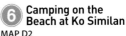

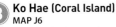

Places to Eat on Ko Phi Phi

PRICE CATEGORIES

For a three-course meal for two with half a bottle of wine (or equivalent meal), taxes, and extra charges.

B under B500 **BB** B500–1,000
BBB over B1,000

 1 Tonsai Village Market
MAP M6 ■ Tonsai Village
■ Open 7am–10pm daily ■ B

Feast on a huge variety of Thai dishes for an unbeatably low price. Try the meat and seafood skewers, or the sweet and savory donuts.

2 Aroy Kaffiene
MAP L6 ■ Tonsai Village
■ 095 720 3382 ■ Open 8am–10pm ■ B

Quaint and charming, Aroy Kaffiene is a small restaurant that serves delicious Thai and international food, imported beers and good coffee.

3 Only Noodles
MAP M6 ■ Tonsai Village
■ Open 10:30am–10:30pm daily ■ B

This no-frills street stall is popular with both locals and visitors. It specializes in noodles paired with meat, seafood, or vegetables.

4 Carpe Diem
MAP M6 ■ Eastern Tonsai
■ Open 10am–midnight daily ■ BB

Located at Phi Phi Village Resort, this beachside restaurant serves Thai and Western favorites. At night, Carpe Diem goes into party mode with cocktail buckets and fire shows.

5 Jasmin BBQ Restaurant
MAP L5 ■ Laem Tong Beach
■ 086 277 0959 ■ Open 10am–10pm daily ■ B

Visit the quiet northern tip of the island for the charmingly unpretentious Jasmine. It's not fancy cooking, but the Thai and Italian food served here is delicious.

6 Cosmic
MAP M6 ■ Tonsai ■ B

Delicious pizzas from a wood-fired oven, homemade pastas, and Thai food attract hungry hordes to this popular restaurant.

Characterful interior of Cosmic

7 Pum Restaurant and Cooking School
MAP M6 ■ Tonsai ■ 081 521 8904
■ Open 11am–9pm daily (classes from 1:30pm) ■ www.pumthai foodchain.com ■ B

Not only can you eat delicious Thai food here, but you can also learn how to make it in the cookery school.

8 Papaya
MAP M6 ■ Tonsai ■ 09115 72007
■ Open 10am–10:30pm daily ■ B

This popular place serves curries, *somtam* (spicy papaya salad), and *pad thai* (stir-fried rice noodles).

9 Efe
MAP M6 ■ Tonsai Village ■ 09515 04434 ■ Open noon–10pm daily ■ BB

Enjoy kebab and *köfte* (meatball) plates at this Mediterranean restaurant.

10 Anna's Restaurant
MAP M6 ■ Tonsai Village
■ 085 923 2596 ■ Open 10:30am–4pm & 5:30–10pm daily ■ B

This clean and efficient restaurant serves both European and Thai food. Local dishes are made spicy, unless requested otherwise.

See map on p98

Streetsmart

Beautifully restored Sino-Portuguese
shop house in old Phuket Town

Getting Around

Arriving by Air

Most travelers to Phuket arrive by air. **Phuket International Airport** (HKT) receives daily direct flights from Australia, North America, Europe, and throughout Asia. These international routes are served by Thailand's national carrier, **Thai Airways**, big-name international and budget airlines, and charter flights. An even greater number of flights arrive at Phuket from destinations within Thailand, including Surat Thani, Bangkok, Chiang Mai, Ko Samui, Utapao (Pattaya), Udorn Thani, and Hat Yai. Airlines include **Air Asia**, **Nok Air**, and **Bangkok Airways**. The flight from Bangkok to Phuket only takes about 90 minutes.

Phuket International Airport is located in the northern part of the island, about 30 minutes' drive from Phuket Town, or an hour from the major southern beaches. The mainland beaches in Phang Nga province north of Phuket, such as Khao Lak, are even closer.

Arriving by Road

Phuket is linked to the mainland by the short Sarasin Bridge, making it easy to travel to the island by car, taxi, or public transportation. There are frequent bus services between Phuket and all major towns in Thailand. Buses between Bangkok and Phuket take around 12 hours, while the journey from Chiang Mai takes 20 hours. It's worth booking reclining seats for these long rides. Minivans also run between Phuket and cities on the mainland, but the bus is preferable for safety and comfort.

Long-distance buses arrive at **Phuket Bus Terminal 2**, located 3 miles (5 km) north of town. From here there are connections by various modes of transportation to every part of the island. The closest train station to Phuket is in Hat Yai, an 8-hour bus ride or a 30-minute flight away from Phuket.

When considering a bus trip, compare prices with the budget airlines – depending on the season, the bus is not always the best value, although it is certainly more scenic.

Arriving by Sea

Passenger ferries, water taxis, speedboats, and private charters arrive at the **Rassada Port** from Ko Phi Phi, Krabi, Trang, Ko Lanta, and Ko Lipe. An international ferry also runs between the port and Langkawi Island in Malaysia, with connections to Penang. Rassada Port is just a 10-minute taxi ride away from Phuket Town.

Getting Around by Car

If you plan to travel widely around Phuket, you might want to consider renting a car. Rates start around B1,500 per day in peak season, but are cheaper in low season. Reputable agencies, such as **Avis**, **Budget**, and **Pure Car Rent**, are located at the airport, in Phuket Town, and at the beaches. Avoid streetside operations.

Valid comprehensive insurance, an International Driving Permit, and seat belts are mandatory, and drink-driving laws are strictly enforced.

Traffic conditions are daunting for the uninitiated, so renting a car with a local driver is often the best option.

Taxis

Metered taxis are easy to find at the airport, but elsewhere they are few and far between, so it is essential to negotiate a fare in advance. Near major taxi stations, signboards will display a list of the maximum fares to a range of destinations, but it's always advisable to verify the fare with the driver before getting into the car. A government crackdown on illegal taxis has made the situation better, but it's still important to avoid pressure from drivers – don't be rushed into a cab, and make sure that the fare is clearly understood. If you meet a driver you like, get their cell phone number and call them when you need a lift. Alternatively, you can use ride-hailing apps, such as **Grab Taxi** and **Bolt**.

Songthaews

Songthaews (pickup trucks with a row of center-facing benches running down each side) offer an inexpensive way of traveling between towns. Rides start from about B20 per person for short distances. Journeys from Phuket Town to various beaches cost about B50–100 per person. *Songthaews* can also be chartered to any destination, and will wait to take you back.

Minivans

Minivans are similar to *songthaews*, but they are not open air, ply more fixed routes (such as the Phuket Bus Terminal to all the beaches), don't stop for passengers to get off and on as frequently, and cannot be chartered. The routes and stops are not always clear, so ask for local advice.

Tuk-Tuk

Unlike in Bangkok, where the tuk-tuk is ubiquitous, these familiar three-wheeled vehicles are no longer used on Phuket. However, small red trucks with open sides, almost like miniature *songthaews*, are often referred to as tuk-tuks. As they tend to be not much cheaper than a taxi, and drivers may take you to tourist traps belonging to friends, it's better to avoid them.

Motorbike Taxis

A fast and easy way to cover short distances is by motorbike taxi. These taxis congregate in the island's most densely populated areas, such as Phuket Town and Patong, and are easily distinguished by their drivers' brightly colored vests.

The cost per person starts at around B20, but negotiate a price beforehand. Always wear a helmet – drivers are required by law to provide one for all passengers.

Boats

Long-tail boats can be chartered along the east coast to visit the islands in Phang Nga Bay, while speedboats depart from Rassada Port. Speedboats and long-tails boats can also be found on southern and west-coast beaches. The long-tail boat drivers usually post their rates on signboards, but these are usually negotiable. The cost to charter should be roughly B500 per hour.

Motorbikes and Bicycles

A cost-effective way of seeing Phuket, motorbiking allows you to travel as you please. Rentals start at around B200 per day for an automatic bike. Be cautious while riding a motorcycle here – always wear a helmet and carry a valid International Driving Permit. Poilice perform spot-checks and will fine you if you do not have the right equipment or license.

Practice defensive riding, since roads are often winding, traffic signage unreliable, and local driving skills treacherous. If you have never ridden a motorbike before, don't start here.

Phuket is mountainous, but some areas, such as the western beaches, are ideal for easy cycling. Bicycles can be rented for about B100 per day.

Walking

Phuket is a very walkable island. In urban and resort areas, sidewalks are plentiful and many streets are pedestrianized, while the countryside is laced with hiking trails. Favorite routes include Nai Harn Beach to Phromthep Cape and Surin Beach to Kamala (see pp52–3).

(see pp52–3)

DIRECTORY

ARRIVING BY AIR

Air Asia
W airasia.com

Bangkok Airways
W bangkokair.com

Nok Air
W nokair.com

Phuket International Airport
W phuketairportthai.com

Thai Airways
W thaiairways.com

ARRIVING BY ROAD

Phuket Bus Terminal 2
Thepkrasattri Road, Ratsada, Muang
C 07637 3193

ARRIVING BY SEA

Rassada Port
Moo 1, Tambon Rassada, Muang
W phuketferry.com

GETTING AROUND BY CAR

Avis
W avis.com

Budget
W budget.co.th

Pure Car Rent
W purecarrent.com

GETTING AROUND BY TAXI

Bolt
W bolt.cu

Grab Taxi
W grab.com/th

Practical Information

Passports and Visas

For entry requirements, including visas, consult your nearest Thai embassy or check the Thai **Ministry of Foreign Affairs** website.

All visitors to Thailand must have a passport valid for six months from the date of entry. Most visitors, including citizens of the UK, US, Australia, and the EU, can enter Thailand for up to 30 days without a pre-arranged visa. For longer visits, apply at the nearest Thai embassy for a tourist visa, which must be used within three months of issue. Non-immigrant 90-day visas are available if there is a good reason for an extended stay, such as education or business. For a fee, 30- or 60-day visas can be extended by 30 days at the Phuket **Immigration Office**. If you overstay your visa, there is a B500 fine per day. These regulations are subject to change.

Many countries, including **Australia**, the **UK**, and the **US** have consular representation in Thailand.

Government Advice

Now more than ever, it is important to consult both your and the Thai government's advice before travelling. The **UK Foreign, Commonwealth and Development Office**, the **US Department of State**, the **Australian Department of Foreign Affairs and Trade**, and the **Royal Thai Government**

offer the latest information on security, health, and local regulations.

Customs Information

You can find information on the laws relating to goods and currency taken in or out of Thailand on the **Thai Customs Department** website. There are strict regulations around the export of antiques and Buddha images.

Insurance

We recommend that you take out a comprehensive insurance policy covering theft, loss of belongings, medical care, delays, and cancellations, and read the small print carefully.

Health

Medical care is excellent and generally inexpensive but, as Thailand does not have reciprocal health agreements with other countries, it's important to take out comprehensive insurance. For serious ailments and surgery, contact **Bangkok Hospital Phuket** or the **Phuket International Hospital**. In an emergency, call the **Medical Hotline**.

For minor ailments, local clinics are hygienic and reliable, and staff generally speak relatively good English. Pharmacies are usually well stocked, and prescriptions are not needed for antibiotics. Nonetheless, if you require a specific medication, ensure you bring a supply with you, with

prescription labels. Dental care is also good and inexpensive.

Stomach upsets caused by unfamiliarity with the food, or contaminated water, are common. Choose food stalls that are popular with locals.

Acclimatization to the sometimes oppressive humidity and heat of Thailand can often take longer than expected. It is wise to drink plenty of bottled water, rest in the shade, and avoid the midday sun for the first few days.

There are no legal immunization requirements unless you are traveling from a country known to be infected with yellow fever. However, it is a good idea to be immunized against polio, tetanus, typhoid, and hepatitis A. BCG (tuberculosis), hepatitis B, rabies, diphtheria, and Japanese encephalitis vaccinations are recommended for people visiting rural areas. Check the latest vaccination requirements with your doctor 4–6 weeks before traveling.

For information regarding COVID-19 vaccination requirements, consult government advice.

Smoking, Alcohol, and Drugs

Smoking is officially prohibited in indoor public areas, although some restaurants and bars do have designated areas for smoking indoors. Importation or sale of e-cigarettes is illegal.

Thailand has a limit of 0.50mg/l of alcohol when driving, and fines for crossing the limit can be harsh.

Possession of illegal drugs, including cannabis, can risk a long prison sentence in Thailand.

ID

By law you must carry photo identification at all times. A photocopy of your passport photo page and visa page is acceptable and means you can leave your passport in a safe place.

Personal Security

Though traveling in Thailand is generally safe, there are some precautions that should be followed. Bag-snatching from passing motorcycles and pick-pocketing are common in Phuket, so it's best to avoid carrying large sums of money and expensive smartphones, or wearing much jewelry. It is advisable to leave your passport and valuables in a safe place, rather than carrying them around. In case of emergency contact the **Tourist Police,** which has an English-speaking operator. Lines are open from 8am to midnight.

Homosexuality was made legal in Thailand in 1956. Thai culture is accepting of the LGBTQ+ community but the law does not yet recognize same-sex marriages or civil unions. There is a vibrant LGBTQ+ scene in Phuket, especially around Patong, but rural areas of the island may be more conservative.

Utopia Asia is a good source of information for LGBTQ+ travelers visiting Thailand.

Travelers with Specific Requirements

Thailand is improving wheelchair accessibility, with many hotels and department stores providing ramps and elevators, but it still has a long way to go. In Phuket, sidewalks are high and uneven, there are few audio signals for visually impaired travelers at traffic crossings, and public transportation is inaccessible. Hiring a car and driver, or visiting the country with a specialized tour agency that can cater to your requirements, such as **Wheelchair Holidays Thailand**, might be the best option.

DIRECTORY

PASSPORTS AND VISAS

Australian Consulate-General, Phuket
MAP K2 ■ 77/77 Chalermprakiat Rama 9 Road
w phuket.consulate.gov.au

Immigration Office
MAP Q6 ■ 482 Phuket Road, Phuket Town
■ 07622 1905

Thai Ministry of Foreign Affairs
w mfa.go.th

UK Embassy, Bangkok
14 Wireless Road
w ukinthailand.fco.gov.uk

US Embassy, Bangkok
95 Wireless Road
w th.usembassy.gov

GOVERNMENT ADVICE

Australian Department of Foreign Affairs and Trade
w dfat.gov.au
w smartraveller.gov.au

Royal Thai Government
w thaigov.go.th

UK Foreign, Commonwealth and Development Office
w gov.uk/foreign-travel-advice

US Department of State
w travel.state.gov

CUSTOMS INFORMATION

Thai Customs Department
w customs.go.th

HEALTH

Bangkok Hospital Phuket
MAP K2 ■ Soi Hongyok Utis, Phuket Town
w phukethospital.com

Medical Hotline
■ 1669

Phuket International Hospital
MAP K2 ■ 44 Chalermprakiat Ror 9 Road
w phuketinternational hospital.com

PERSONAL SECURITY

Tourist Police
■ 1155

Utopia Asia
w utopia-asia.com

TRAVELERS WITH SPECIFIC REQUIREMENTS

Wheelchair Holidays Thailand
w wheelchairtours.com

Time Difference

Thailand is three hours behind Australian Eastern Standard Time, seven hours ahead of Greenwich Mean Time, and eleven hours ahead of US Eastern Standard Time. Daylight saving time is not observed.

Money

Thailand's currency is the baht (B). Foreign currency may be accepted, but the rate of exchange will not be favorable. Most establishments accept major credit, debit, and prepaid currency cards, though it is always a good idea to carry cash for small transactions.

Tipping is not customary in Thailand but a small tip as a mark of appreciation is welcome nonetheless. The following amounts are recommended as a guideline: 20 baht per person served in a restaurant; 20 baht per bag for a hotel porter; 100 baht for the concierge; round up taxi fares to the nearest 10 baht.

Electrical Appliances

The electrical current in Thailand flows at 220 volts AC, 50 Hz, and most plug sockets are of the two-pin variety. Adaptors are readily available in department stores.

Cell Phones and Wi-Fi

Thailand uses the GSM 4G cell phone and data system. If you own a GSM cell phone and international roaming is activated, it is easy to make and receive calls, but you might save money by buying a local SIM card.

Free Wi-Fi is available in virtually all accommodations, as well as many restaurants, cafes, and malls, although speeds may not be high.

Postal Services

Thailand has a reliable postal system, and stamps are available at all post offices and at many hotels. Letters to or from Europe or the US usually take a week or longer to arrive. Post offices also offer packing services. For important documents, it is advisable to use the **Express Mail Service (EMS)**, an international courier, or register the letter for an extra fee.

Weather

The climate is at its best from November to February, when skies are clear and temperatures cooler – generally around 80° F (26.5° C). The hot season (March to May) is fine for a beach holiday, but not for sightseeing.During the rainy season (June to October) temperatures are milder, but Phuket still gets plenty of sun.

Opening Hours

Stores generally open at 10am and close at 9pm or 10pm. Government offices are open 8:30am–4:30pm, but many close for lunch. Tourist attractions tend to open 9am–5pm, unless an evening program is on offer. Banks usually work 8:30am–3:30pm, but mini-branches offering money exchange are open later. Post offices work 8:30am–4:30pm Monday–Friday and 9am–noon on Saturday. On public holidays government offices, banks, and post offices are closed, but most stores remain open.

COVID-19 Increased rates of infection may result in temporary opening hours and/or closures. Always check ahead before visiting museums, attractions, and hospitality venues.

Visitor Information

The **Tourism Authority of Thailand**, the official government tourist board, has an office in Phuket Town, offering maps, brochures, and advice. Its website has details on destinations and events throughout Thailand.

Several commercial websites provide up-to-date reviews of attractions in Phuket. One of the best of these, **Phuket.com**, is a mine of information on the island's beaches, restaurants, and nightlife.

If you are planning on visiting the island's national parks, the **Department of National Parks** has a website with useful information on planning trips, including reserving park accommodations. Visitor centers at Khao Phra Thaeo Royal Forest and Wildlife Reserve (see pp20–21), Sirinat National Park (see pp22–3), and Khao Sok National Park (see pp32–5) also offer maps, guides, and other useful services.

Trips and Tours

Phuket offers a wide variety of specialist trips and tours. Water-sport excursions are very popular. **Phuket Dive Tours** offers day trips and live-aboard boats, which visit popular dive sites, such as the Similan Islands. Charter companies and yacht clubs, such as **Phuket Sail Tours,** offer day trips and overnight tours. Alternatively, explore the lagoons of Phang Nga Bay by kayak with **John Gray's Sea Canoe** (see p37).

On dry land, **Amazing Bike Tours Thailand** (see p55) offers cycling trips to Khao Lak and Khao Sok National Park, and **Blue Elephant Cooking School** teaches Thai recipes.

Local Customs

Thais are known for their tolerance, amiability, and helpfulness. Nonetheless, there are a few local values to bear in mind. Direct confrontation and aggressive behavior are considered particularly inappropriate. The monarchy, past and present, is protected by local reverence and strict laws, so avoid any mention of the royal family.

The head is considered a sacred part of the body, so do not touch people's heads, and avoid pointing your feet (which are considered lowly) at people or religious icons when seated.

Always remove your shoes when entering a home. Wearing ultrashort shorts or skirts, and men and women going topless in public, are all considered impolite.

Visiting Buddhist Temples

Visitors are welcome in Thai wats, but should act respectfully, and dress modestly. Shorts and sleeveless shirts are not appropriate, and shoes should be removed before entering. Greet monks with a smile and a nod. Women are not permitted to hand anything directly to a monk.

Language

The official language in Thailand is Thai, but basic English is widespread, although not guaranteed. Cell phone apps offering voice to voice translation can come in handy.

Taxes and Refunds

Thailand imposes a 7 per cent Value Added Tax (VAT) on goods and services. There is a VAT refund scheme for visitors who are in the country for less than 180 days. Look out for shops displaying a "VAT Refund for Tourists" sign and show your passport to the sales assistant who will fill out a VAT refund form, which you will need to present to the customs desk at the airport before departure.

Accommodations

In Phuket, there is a huge variety of accommodations, from luxury villas to dorm rooms. It's even possible to stay in a tent on Mai Khao beach in the Sirinat National Park. Patong's simple hostels suit its nightlife-lovers, while 5-star resorts abound in the Cherngtalay area. Kata is the best mid-priced beach option.

The high tourist season, when prices are higher and rooms should be reserved in advance, is between November and May. Prices are partiularly high between Christmas and New Year. Ask about reduced tariffs during the low season, between June and October. Many accommodations post their rates online.

DIRECTORY

POSTAL SERVICES

Express Mail Service (EMS)

w ems.post

VISITOR INFORMATION

Department of National Parks

w park.dnp.go.th

Phuket.com

w phuket.com

Tourism Authority of Thailand

MAP P5 ▪ 191 Thalang Road, Phuket Town

w tourismthailand.org

TRIPS AND TOURS

Blue Elephant Cooking School

w blueelephant cookingschool.com

Phuket Dive Tours

w phuketdivetours.com

Phuket Sail Tours

w phuketdivetours.com

Places to Stay

> **PRICE CATEGORIES**
> For a standard, double room per night (with breakfast if included), taxes, and extra charges.
> ....
> **B** under B3,000 **BB** B3,000–6,000 **BBB** over B6,000

Luxury Hotels

Dusit Thani Laguna Phuket

MAP B6 ▪ 390/1 Moo 1, Srisoonthorn Road, Cherngtalay ▪ 07636 2999 ▪ www.dusit.com ▪ BB

Located in the Laguna Phuket Resort complex, this hotel is set in tropical gardens fronting onto the lovely Bang Tao Beach. It offers its guests access to numerous Laguna facilities, including an 18-hole golf course.

JW Marriott Phuket Resort & Spa

MAP B2 ▪ 231 Moo 3, Mai Khao Beach ▪ 07633 8000 ▪ www.marriott.com ▪ BB

Rated as one of Asia's top luxury resorts, the Phuket Marriott was among the first high-end properties to be developed along the island's northwest coast. The guest rooms feature wooden floors, silks, and plush bedding.

Sala Phuket Resort & Spa

MAP B2 ▪ M333 Moo 3, Mai Khao Beach ▪ 07633 8888 ▪ www.salaresorts.com ▪ BB

This ultrastylish boutique resort on Mai Khao Beach is set in gorgeous natural surroundings with five-star facilities. The design marries a classic Phuket architectural style with all modern conveniences.

Amanpuri

MAP A6 ▪ Pansea Beach ▪ 07632 4333 ▪ www.amanresorts.com ▪ BBB

Graceful, traditional Thai architecture harmonizes with the magnificent tropical surroundings at this luxurious resort. Villas come in Thai-style pavilions, pool pavilions, and villa homes. Located on the exclusive Pansea Beach, Amanpuri has five top-rated restaurants, including the French-Japanese Naoki, which is open November to April.

Anantara Mai Khao Phuket Villas

MAP B2 ▪ 888 Moo 3, Mai Khao Beach ▪ 07633 6100 ▪ www.phuket.anantara.com ▪ BBB

High levels of privacy and comfort await at these private villas. Rooms feature sliding glass doors that open directly onto your own private swimming pool, while tall fences and greenery guarantee maximum seclusion.

The Sarojin

MAP F2 ▪ 60 Moo 2 Kukkak, Takuapa, Phang Nga ▪ 076 4279 004 ▪ www.sarojin.com ▪ BBB

Developed in an Asian design style, this luxury resort has 56 guest residences. Sheltered by Pakarang Cape, a coral headland, the resort's lovely beach offers calm swimming conditions all the year round. For the ultimate in romance, book a private dinner for two by a candlelit waterfall.

Six Senses Yao Noi

MAP F3 ▪ 56 Moo 5, Ko Yao Noi ▪ 07641 8500 ▪ www.sixsenses.com ▪ BBB

Located on a picturesque island in Phang Nga Bay, this luxury hideaway features lush tropical gardens. Each of the resorts's 54 sumptuous villas has its own pool. The resort also offers a range of excursions and activities.

Sri Panwa

MAP K5 ▪ 31/17 Moo 8, Sakdidej Road ▪ 07637 1000–3 ▪ www.sripanwa.com ▪ BBB

With breathtaking views from atop Panwa Cape, on the southeast coast of Phuket, Sri Panwa's villas are set amid lush tropical surroundings. They are designed in a contemporary tropical style and many of the rooms feature 360-degree views.

The Surin Phuket

MAP A6 ▪ 118 Moo 3, Pansea Beach ▪ 07631 6400 ▪ www.thesurinphuket.com ▪ BBB

This luxury resort features 108 well-designed suites and cottages scattered around the beach, pool, and coconut groves. The cottages have handcrafted teakwood floors, private verandas, and secluded sun decks. Located on Pansea Bay, in the upscale Cherngtalay area, the Surin Phuket enjoys spectacular views.

Zeavola

MAP L4 ▪ Moo 8 Laem Tong, Ko Phi Phi ▪ 07562 7000 ▪ www.zeavola. com ▪ BBB

This luxury resort is situated on Ko Phi Phi Don's northern tip. The resort's 53 guest bungalows are fashioned out of rich Thai teakwood, and the beds feature cool linens. The resort offers a speedboat transfer service from Phuket.

Boutique Hotels

Baan Yin Dee

MAP N2 ▪ 7/5 Muean Ngen Road, Patong Beach ▪ 07636 4591–3 ▪ www.baanyindee.com ▪ BB

This resort has Thai-style architecture and decorative finishes. On a hill above Patong, the rooftop terrace has great views and benefits from a breeze, while the pools are perfect for a cool dip. Rooms feature wooden floors and gentle lighting.

Chanalai Flora Resort

MAP H5 ▪ 175 Koktanode Road, Kata Beach ▪ 07633 0148 ▪ www.chanalai. com ▪ BB

A modern-style resort hotel located just five minutes from the beach. The rooms are spacious, and most have balconies. The resort has two swimming pools and also provides free Wi-Fi.

Impiana Resort Phuket

MAP N2 ▪ 41 Thaweewong Road, Patong Beach ▪ 07634 0138 ▪ www. impiana.com ▪ BB

This seaside resort enjoys access to the area's

nightlife venues, fine restaurant, and attractions. If you wish to retire somewhere peaceful, the gates to this resort transport you into a true oasis.

The Nai Harn

MAP H5 ▪ 23/3 Vises Road, Nai Harn Beach ▪ 07638 0200–10 ▪ www. thenaiharn.com ▪ BB

The views of Nai Harn Bay from this beachfront property are breathtaking, and it is also the only hotel with direct access to the beach. The rooftop pool bar, Reflections, offers 360-degree views.

The Old Phuket

MAP H4 ▪ 192/36 Karon Road, Karon ▪ 07639 6353-6 ▪ www.theold phuket.com ▪ BB

Designed in the classic Phuket architectural style that was popular on the island in the 19th century, this charming hotel still retains the glory of the island's tin-mining days. The rooms are modern, with clean lines; some have private Jacuzzis.

Aleenta Resort & Spa

MAP E2 ▪ 33 Moo 5, Kok Klooy, Takuatung, Phang Nga ▪ 07658 0333 ▪ www.aleenta.com/ phuket ▪ BBB

Located 20 minutes north of Phuket airport, Aleenta offers bright and airy rooms. For the ultimate in exclusivity, book a beachfront villa, which comes with a personal butler.

Keemala

MAP G1 ▪ Nakasud Road, Kamala ▪ 07635 8777 www.keemala.com ▪ BBB

Nestled in an old-growth forest hillside, set above Kamala Bay, each of the

38 villas has a different character, from tree houses to safari tents to thatched-roof pavilions, all done with imagination and sophistication. The ethos is wellness, with healthy food, a superb spa and yoga classes.

Malisa Villa Suites

MAP H5 ▪ 40/36 Kata Road, Kata Beach ▪ 07628 4760-4 ▪ www.malisa villas.com ▪ BBB

The resort's name derives from the Thai word for jasmine. The rooms, designed to evoke the comforts of home with modern kitchens and comfortable living spaces, open onto private pools.

Paresa Resort

MAP G1 ▪ 49 Moo 6, Layi-Nakalay Road, Kamala ▪ 07630 2000 ▪ www. paresaresorts.com ▪ BBB

Paresa is perched atop a cliff overlooking the Andaman Sea, between Patong and Kamala bays and surrounded by trees and flowers. This secluded boutique resort features spacious villas, many with private pools.

Phi Phi Island Village Beach Resort

MAP F3 ▪ 97/197–9 Moo 4, Virat Hongyok Road, Ko Phi Phi ▪ 07562 8900 ▪ www.phiphiisland village.com ▪ BBB

The villas and thatched roof bungalows of this resort blend well with Ko Phi Phi Don's tropical terrain. The interiors feature rich teakwood and comfortable luxury furnishings. The resort also has its own private beach, as well as a pool overlooking Lo Ba Goa Bay and the Andaman Sea.

Twinpalms Phuket

MAP A6 ▪ 106/46 Moo 3, Surin Beach Road ▪ 07631 6500 ▪ www.twinpalms-phuket.com ▪ BBB

The sleek, minimalist rooms at Twinpalms are personalized with local decorative touches and bespoke furniture. The grounds feature tranquil and imaginative tropical water gardens.

Romantic Hotels

Cape Panwa Hotel

MAP K5 ▪ 27 Moo 8, Sakdidej Road, Cape Panwa ▪ 07639 1123–5 ▪ www.capepanwa.com ▪ BB

A charming property on Phuket's southeastern coast, this hotel has hosted many Hollywood film stars, while the classic Panwa House, now a restaurant, is regularly featured in movies. The hotel also has a spa, as well as access to a private beach.

Sawasdee Village Resort and Spa

MAP H5 ▪ 38 Katekwan Road, Kata Beach ▪ 07633 0979 ▪ www.phuket sawasdee.com ▪ BB

Designed to resemble a traditional Thai village, using teakwood and Thai art and artifacts, this resort has been named one of the most beautiful in the country.

Andara Resort and Villas

MAP G1 ▪ 15 Moo 6, Kamala ▪ 07633 8777 ▪ www.andaraphuket.com ▪ BBB

Set on a gently sloping hillside overlooking the Andaman Sea, this luxury Thai-inspired retreat features spacious and luxurious villas as well as suites, with sea views and private infinity pools. Andara Resort's restaurant, Silk *(see p66)*, serves the finest Thai cuisine in stylish surroundings.

Banyan Tree

MAP B6 ▪ 33/27 Moo 4, Srisoonthorn Road, Cherngtalay ▪ 07637 2400 ▪ www.banyantree.com ▪ BBB

Located in the upscale Laguna resorts complex, this marvelous resort exudes romance and charm. Guests of the hotel can opt to take a dinner cruise on *Sanya Rak* ("promise of love"), an aptly named vessel for experiencing Phuket's legendary sunsets.

JW Marriott Khao Lak Resort & Spa

MAP E1 ▪ 41/12 Moo 3, Khuk Khak, Takua Pa, Phang Nga ▪ 07658 4888 ▪ www.marriott.com ▪ BBB

A popular destination for honeymooners, this beachfront resort north of Phuket island features Southeast Asia's longest swimming pool. Nearby attractions include parks, waterfalls, and scuba diving sites.

Mom Tri's Villa Royale Phuket

MAP H5 ▪ 12 Kata Noi Road, Kata Noi Beach ▪ 07633 3568 ▪ www.villaroyalephuket.com ▪ BBB

This boutique hotel, a former royal summer house, features luxurious suites decorated with traditional Thai artistic touches. One of its three pools is carved into the seashore rocks and filled with seawater. The property's private cruiser, *Yacht Royale*, provides exclusive day trips to Phang Nga Bay.

The Pavilions Phuket

MAP B6 ▪ 31/1 Moo 6, Cherngtalay ▪ 07631 7600 ▪ www.pavilionshotels.com ▪ BBB

The romantic villas at this resort offer either ocean or hillside views, with unequaled privacy. Rooms all have modern Asian interiors with European touches. It also has facilities for weddings.

The Slate Phuket

MAP B4 ▪ Nai Yang Beach ▪ 07632 7006 ▪ www.the slatephuket.com ▪ BBB

This bold property uses raw timber and modern chic to stunning effect. Suites feature subtle touches of individual artistry and have gentle lighting. The villas with private pools offer the ultimate in romantic seclusion, and the spa has treatments-for-two rooms. The hotel has received numerous awards for its trend-setting design.

Trisara Phuket Resort

MAP B6 ▪ 60/1 Moo 6, Srisoonthorn Road, Cherngtalay ▪ 07631 0100 ▪ www.trisara.com ▪ BBB

Located on a private bay and set among lush tropical foliage, Trisara offers 39 private pool villas and suites with an emphasis on privacy. Dedicated cooks and service staff cater to your every need.

Mid-Range Hotels

Baan Krating

MAP H6 ▪ 11/3 Moo 1, Wiset Road, Rawai, Ao Sane Beach ▪ 07651 0927 ▪ www.baankrating.com ▪ B

With a lush jungle setting, Baan Krating is a haven of seclusion and peace. The villas are well appointed, clean, and comfortable. The beach bar overlooks Nai Harn Bay.

Metropole Phuket

MAP P5 ▪ 1 Soi Surin, Montri Road, Phuket Town ▪ 07621 4020 ▪ www.metropolephuket. com ▪ B

The Metropole Phuket offers 248 rooms and suites in Phuket Town. Guests can enjoy traditional Thai-style spa massages, or dine in the two restaurants or in the executive cocktail lounge.

The Royal Palm Beach Front

MAP N1 ▪ 66/2 Thaweewong Road, Patong ▪ 07634 2424 ▪ www. theroyalpalm.com ▪ B

Smart interiors define the 67 rooms at the Royal Palm, located in the heart of Patong. With a range of facilities, including an outdoor pool and Jacuzzi, a steam room, and a spa, the hotel offers travelers many comforts.

Sino House

MAP P5 ▪ 1 Montri Road, Phuket Town ▪ 076 232 494 ▪ www.sinohouse phuket.com ▪ B

Sino House is a modern three story building, near the Old Town area, nicely decorated and furnished in Sino-Portuguese style. Rooms are large and airy, with floor-to-ceiling windows overlooking a pretty garden.

Baan Laimai Beach Resort

MAP N1 ▪ 66 Thaweewong Road, Patong ▪ 07634 2620 ▪ www. baanlaimai.com ▪ BB

This resort offers privacy in the heart of Patong. Some rooms feature hardwood floors and Asian-inspired design. The swimming pool encircles an island with palm trees, accessed via a charming bridge.

Burasari Patong Boutique Hotel

MAP N2 ▪ 18/110 Ruamjai Road, Patong ▪ 07629 2929 ▪ www. burasari.com ▪ BB

Named after the rare flower that blooms on the property, this hotel offers tranquility and rooms decorated in an elegant classic northern Thai Lanna (traditional style) fashion.

Kamala Beach Resort

MAP G1 ▪ 96/42–3, Moo 3, Kamala Beach, Kathu, Phuket ▪ 07634 2620 ▪ www.kamalabeach.com ▪ BB

Located close to the beach, the weekend market, and good restaurants, this resort has four pools, a massage parlour, and a gym. Guests must be over 16 years of age.

Kata Palm Resort and Spa

MAP H5 ▪ 60 Kata Road, Kata ▪ 07628 4334–8 ▪ www.katapalmresort. com ▪ BB

The comfortable rooms are furnished in Thai wood and fabrics, with hand-carved teak decorations. With Karon and Kata nearby, guests are close to great shopping, dining, and nightlife.

Manathai Surin

MAP A6 ▪ 121 Srisoonthorn Road, Surin ▪ 07636 0250 ▪ www. manathai.com ▪ BB

A stylish boutique hotel on Surin Beach, Manathai blends contemporary architectural design with classic Asian styles, textures, and fabrics. The spa offers a range of therapeutic massages, scrubs, and wraps.

Mangosteen Resort & Spa

MAP J5 ▪ 99/4 Moo 7, Soi Mangosteen, Rawai ▪ 07628 9399 ▪ www. mangosteen-phuket.com ▪ BB

A peaceful hilltop resort, the Mangosteen enjoys lovely views of the hills, beaches, and bays of Phuket. At night there's a free shuttle service to the nearby Rawai and Nai Harn beaches. It also offers an Ayurveda and wellness spa.

Millennium Resort

MAP N2 ▪ 199 Rat Uthit 200 Pee Road, Patong ▪ 07660 1999 ▪ www. millenniumhotels.com ▪ BB

Located off the beach in Patong, this resort gets high marks from visitors for its location. It is next to the upscale Jungceylon shopping mall, and also surrounded by popular restaurants and vibrant nightlife. Rooms range from simple chic studios to expansive suites.

For a key to hotel price categories see p112

Family Hotels

Hilton Phuket Arcadia Resort & Spa

MAP H4 ▪ 333 Patak Road, Karon ▪ 07639 6433 ▪ www.hilton.com ▪ BB

This is a vast, tropical garden complex on Karon beach, with multiple pools and tennis and squash courts, as well as a choice of ten resorts. The hotel also offers the Kidz Paradise club, with a team of professionals to keep the children happy while parents are enjoying the spa, gym, or beach.

Holiday Inn Resort Phuket

MAP N2 ▪ 52 Thaweewong Road, Patong ▪ 07637 0200 ▪ phuket.holidayinn resorts.com ▪ BB

With specially designed family and kids' suites, this resort also has an extensive Kids Club for children under 12. Club 12, a parent-free zone with Internet, games, movies, and karaoke, is perfect for teenagers.

Laguna Holiday Club Resort

MAP B6 ▪ 61 Moo 4, Srisoonthorn Road, Cherngtalay ▪ 07627 1888 ▪ www.laguna holidayclubresort.com ▪ BB

An all-suite resort, this is the most kid-friendly option in the sedate Laguna area. The Kids Club organizes painting and mask-making events, treasure hunts, bowling, and an introduction to Thai games and crafts. Kids over eight can take scuba lessons; babysitting facilities are available.

Phuket Graceland Resort & Spa

MAP N1 ▪ 190 Thaweewong Road, Patong ▪ 07637 0500 ▪ www.phuketgraceland. com ▪ BB

The Graceland Resort's Kids Club gives children a supervised place in which to play and watch movies. There is also a bowling alley, swimming pool, and a Jacuzzi.

Angsana Laguna Phuket

MAP B6 ▪ Srisoonthorn Road, Cherngtalay ▪ 07635 8500 ▪ www. angsana.com ▪ BBB

Aside from the expansive grounds (perfect for cycling) and the ocean- and lagoon-based water-sports (sailing and paddle boarding), the Angsana's Tree House Kids Club gets top reviews. Even the spa has a specially tailored children's menu.

Katathani Phuket Beach Resort

MAP H4 ▪ 14 Kata Noi Road, Karon Beach ▪ 07633 0009 ▪ www. katathani.com ▪ BBB

Situated on the secluded Kata Noi Bay, this stylish, self-contained luxury beach resort features six outdoor swimming pools, including four specially for kids, sports and crafts classes, a Kids Club, and six restaurants.

Le Meridien Phuket Beach Resort

MAP H4 ▪ 29 Soi Karon Nui, Karon ▪ 07637 0100 ▪ www.starwoodhotels. com ▪ BBB

This resort's Penguin Club for kids aged 3–12 years offers a range of activities. The resort features a mini-golf course, rock-climbing wall, and multiple pools. Children can also learn Thai dancing and ice cream making.

Metadee Resort

MAP H4 ▪ 66 Kata Road, Kata ▪ 07633 7888 ▪ www.metadee phuket. com ▪ BBB

Near Kata Yai Beach, this chic resort has rooms in a unique setting – they are in a garden surrounded by a large pool. As a result, nearly every room enjoys direct access to the water. There is also a special children's pool and a fitness center.

Mövenpick Resort & Spa

MAP H4 ▪ 509 Patak Road, Karon ▪ 07639 6139 ▪ www.moeven pick-hotels.com ▪ BBB

The resort's Play Zone is one of the largest on Phuket. Here, children can participate in a variety of supervised activities.

InterContinental Phuket Resort

MAP G1 ▪ 333 Kamala, Kathu ▪ 07662 9999 ▪ www.phuket.inter continental.com ▪ BBB

Set right on Kamala Beach, this family-friendly luxury hotel features a great Kids' Club for the little ones, with a roster of daily events. It also has a gym, spa, and beach club for parents.

Renaissance Phuket Resort & Spa

MAP B2 ▪ 555 Moo 3, Mai Khao Beach ▪ 07636 3999 ▪ www.marriott.com ▪ BBB

Surrounded by greenery and featuring a waterslide,

the kids' pool at this resort is a favorite. Away from the water, the Kids Club entertains youngsters with movies, puzzles, books, and video games, all supervised by childcare professionals. The lovely grounds are set within a national park.

Budget Hotels

Andatel Hotel Patong Phuket
MAP N2 ▪ 41/9 Rat Uthit 200 Pee Road, Patong ▪ 07629 0480 ▪ www. andatelhotel.com ▪ B
A short distance from the beach, this hotel has classic Thai-style villas and a charming pool that receives sunlight through the day. Rooms are simple but well kept.

Deevana Patong Resort & Spa
MAP N2 ▪ 43/2 Rat Uthit, 200 Pee Road, Patong ▪ 07634 1414–5 ▪ www. deevanapatong.com ▪ B
This secluded 4-star resort, surrounded by tropical gardens, sprawls across 12 acres (5 ha) of land in Patong. On your doorstep, however, are the island's best nightlife, fine dining, and entertainment venues. Simple, clean guest rooms are tastefully decorated and quite comfortable.

Good 9 @ Home
MAP H6 ▪ Soi Wassana, Viset Road, Rawai ▪ 081 834 3898 ▪ www.face book.com/good9athome ▪ B
A simple, seven-room guesthouse, Good 9 gets great reviews for cleanliness and friendly staff. The location is very quiet,

yet just a few minutes' walk from Rawai Beach. Book in advance.

Hemingway's Hotel
MAP N3 ▪ 188/17–20 Phangmuang, Patong ▪ 07654 0895 ▪ www. hemingwayshotel.com ▪ B
Named after the larger-than-life American novelist, this hotel is a decadent place to stay. The rooms have rich wood paneling and furniture, lush silk throws and pillows, and tranquil Buddha images. Despite the luxurious furnishings, Hemingway's is good value for money in Patong.

Kata Beach Studio
MAP H4 ▪ 90/5 Khoktanod Road, Kata ▪ 07633 3323 ▪ www.katabeach studio.com ▪ B
Guests can really make themselves at home in these modern studios, which have kitchens and balconies. The rooftop pool and Jacuzzi benefit from impressive views. There is also a swanky poolside bar that is open daily until 10pm.

The Memory at On On Hotel
MAP K3 ▪ 19 Phang Nga Road, Phuket Town ▪ 07621 1154 ▪ B
Phuket Town's oldest hotel, The Memory at On On Hotel still retains a special character and traditional charm despite its tasteful renovation. The affordable dorm rooms feature curtains for privacy. If it looks familiar, a scene from the Leonardo DiCaprio movie *The Beach* was filmed here.

Nai Yang Beach Resort
MAP B3 ▪ 65/23–4 Nai Yang Beach Road ▪ 07632 8300 ▪ B
Located in the heart of Sirinat National Park, the resort promises a relaxing stay at prices that are tough to beat. The scenery is memorable – you drive past a rubber plantation on the way, and the resort is set right on Nai Yang Beach.

Patong Pearl Resortel
MAP N1 ▪ 3 Sawadirak Road, Patong ▪ 07634 0121 ▪ B
With its central location in Patong, this modern and well-maintained hotel is a comfortable place at which to unwind in the middle of the busy city. A swimming pool and sun deck lift the Patong Pearl a cut above other budget properties.

Rattana Beach Hotel
MAP H4 ▪ 72/2–5 Patak Road, Karon ▪ 07639 6415–7 ▪ B
The Rattana offers guests well-priced accommodations close to Karon Beach. Superior rooms have balconies overlooking the pool. Enjoy a cocktail at the poolside bar, or a short stroll to the beach.

White Sand Resortel
MAP N1 ▪ 3–7 Sawadirak Road, Patong ▪ 07629 6013–8 ▪ www.whitesand patong.com ▪ B
Quiet rooms and very spacious suites all come with a private balcony and sea or garden views. The hotel restaurant is well known for its fresh seafood, and there's a rooftop pool.

For a key to hotel price categories see p112

General Index

Acknowledgments

This edition updated by

Contributor Barbara Woolsey
Senior Editor Alison McGill
Senior Designer Vinita Venugopal
Project Editors Dipika Dasgupta, Rebecca Flynn
Art Editor Bandana Paul
Editor Anuroop Sanwalia
Picture Research Administrator Vagisha Pushp
Picture Research Manager Taiyaba Khatoon
Publishing Assistant Halima Mohammed
Jacket Designer Jordan Lambley
Cartographer Ashif
Cartography Manager Suresh Kumar
Senior DTP Designer Tanveer Zaidi
Senior Production Editor Jason Little
Production Controller Manjit Sihra
Deputy Managing Editor Beverly Smart
Managing Editors Shikha Kulkarni, Hollie Teague
Managing Art Editor Sarah Snelling
Senior Managing Art Editor Priyanka Thakur
Art Director Maxine Pedliham
Publishing Director Georgina Dee

DK would like to thank the following for their contribution to the previous editions: Hilary Bird, William Bredesen, Peter Holmshaw, Brent Madison, Neil Ray, Clare Peel

The publisher would like to thank the following for their kind permission to reproduce their photographs:
Key: a-above; b-below/bottom; c-center; f-far; l-left; r-right; t-top

123RF.com: Sergey Belov 76-7; Nilanjan Bhattacharya 77cr; John Hu 74b; milxela 69tl; mklrnt 75br; Patryk Kośmider 100-1; Chirasak Tolertmongkol 20clb.

Alamy Stock Photo: Mary Andrews 84b; Arco Images / Kiedrowski; R. 71tr; Arco Images GmbH / K. Kreder 4cl, 57cl; David Austin 28br; Sergey Belov 4b; Chronicle 41tr; Sorin Colac 36-7; Danita Delimont / Stuart Westmorland 11cr; Gary Dublanko 36cl; Eagle Visions Photography / Craig Lovell 11cb; Chris Fredriksson 82b; Robert Fried 71cl; Kevin Hellon 3tr, 15cra, 92-3, 104-5; Friedrich von Hörsten 30br; imageBROKER / Stella 23tl, 27tl; International Photobank 74tc; ISOPA Images Limited 60t; Kees Metselaar 91t; Jason Knott 12cl, 61cl, 68cla; LOOK Die Bildagentur der Fotografen GmbH / Thomas Stankiewicz 19bl; Craig Lovell 52c; Benny Marty 4t; MediaWorldImages 4clb; MO:SES 4crb; National Geographic Creative 94tr; Ernita Nenggala 54clb; Panther Media GmbH / perszing1982 2tl, 8-9; parasola.net 48-9,

98tl; Chalermpon Poungpeth 60br; Dmitry Rukhlenko - Travel Photos 7br; M. Sobreira 2tr, 38-9, 53br; Solarsys 91br; Samuel Spicer 32clb; travelstock44.de / Juergen Held 48cla; Peter Treanor 19crb; United Archives GmbH 63tr; Peter Vallance 22cl; Steve Vidler 54-5; Matthew Wakem 55tr; Jan Wlodarczyk 42-3b; Andrew Woodley 63c; Zoonar GmbH / Sergey Pristyazhnyuk (Serg Zastavkin) 26crb.

Baan Rim Pa: 87clb.

Banyan Tree Gallery Phuket: 96cr.

Black Ginger: 97cr.

Bridgeman Images: History / Rainer Krack 40t.

Dreamstime.com: Dimitris Apostolou 28-9; Stuart Atkinson 46bc; Babycoconut 14bl; Ihar Balaikin 82tl; Banky405 11tr; Sergey Belov 35b; Pipop Boosarakumwadi 6cla; Tania Castán 100tl; Pakphipat Charoenrach 10cr; Doraclub 23br; Jakob Fischer 76crb; Fabio Formaggio 65tr; Geargodz 95t; Simon Gurney 29br; Sean Harms 16-7; Jaroon Ittiwannapong 73cl; Attila Jandi 35cra; Jedynakanna 102br; Kajornyot 34cr; Sombat Khamin 12-3, 42t; Khellon 11br, 12br, 14t; Patryk Kosmider 33tl; Torsten Kuenzlen 92clb; Ratchanikon Kulaptip 52t; Manit Larpluechai 33crb; Adam Laws 11ca; Chee-onn Leong 10br; Lestor 49cl; Jedsada Luadthainarong 13cr; Thanawut Makawan 18-9; Maria Malkina 26cla; Aliaksandr Mazurkevich 17br; Sophie Mcaulay 70crb; Mosaymay 10cla, 53cl; Mullrich 10clb; Narong Niemhom 81clb, 88–9; Apidech Ninkhlai 4cla; Nokhook 75cla; Kampee Patisena 37clb; Pavantt 26-7; Alexey Pavlov 44t; Wiroj Phongthadaporn 30-1; Pakpoom Phummee 10cra, 15bl, 73tr; Ppy2010ha 67tr; Viacheslav Ryukhko 23clb; Smolny1 29tl, Lee Snider 19tl, 45cr; Nickolay Stanev 20cra; Tayawee Supan 42tl, 68-9; Suriya007 34bl; Suttipong Sutiratanachai 99b; Aleksey Suvorov 62tr; Tagstiles 50b; Thawats 21bl; Artit Thongchuea 32br; Tuayai 17tl; Nuttawut Uttamaharad 27cr; Valentyn75 69b; Yongkiet 3tl, 36br, 78-9.

FLPA: OceanPhoto 31clb.

Getty Images: Pete Atkinson 77tl; Paula Bronstein 41clb; Adisorn Fineday Chutikunakorn 72b; Ashit Desai 72tl; Reinhard Dirscherl 56tl; Michael Freeman 71bl; Gallo Images / Danita Delimont 31br; John Harper 50tl; Martin Harvey 34tl; Kaveh Kazemi 46bl; Lonely Planet Images / Wibowo Rusli 17cr; LOOK-foto / Ingolf Pompe 58-9; 67cl; Moment / Luciana Calvin 101cla, / Sirachai Arunrugstichai 30cl, / Vincent Jary 102cl; Norbert Probst 83cl; Sebun Photo / Youjiro Oda 81tr; Sirachai Arunrugstichai 99tl;

Ullstein Bild / Raimund Franken 56b, 80cla; Ullstein Bild / Reinhard Dirscherl 4cra; 57tr; Stuart Westmorland 54tr.

The Gibbon Rehabilitation Project: 93bl.

Illuzion Phuket: 65cl.

iStockphoto.com: 4FR 24-5; aphotostory 51tl; lkunl 32-3; martinhosmart 1; RoBeDeRo 18clb.

Robert Harding Picture Library: Ingolf Pompe 62b.

Suay: 66bl.

Shutterstock.com: Denis Costille 84tc.

SuperStock: imageBROKER / Josef Beck 94b.

White Box Restaurant: Stefano Beber 66tr.

Cover

Front and spine: **iStockphoto.com:** martinhosmart.

Back: **Alamy Stock Photo:** Hemis tr, imageBROKER cla, Jan Wlodarczyk crb; **Dreamstime.com:** Piyato tl; **iStockphoto.com:** martinhosmart b.

Pull Out Map Cover

iStockphoto.com: martinhosmart.

All other images © Dorling Kindersley
For further information see: www.dkimages.com

Penguin Random House

First edition 2012

Published in Great Britain by Dorling Kindersley Limited
DK, One Embassy Gardens, 8 Viaduct Gardens, London SW11 7BW, UK

The authorised representative in the EEA is Dorling Kindersley Verlag GmbH. Arnulfstr. 124, 80636 Munich, Germany

Published in the United States by DK Publishing, 1745 Broadway, 20th Floor, New York, NY 10019, USA

Copyright © 2012, 2022 Dorling Kindersley Limited

A Penguin Random House Company

22 23 24 25 10 9 8 7 6 5 4 3 2 1

A CIP catalog record is available from the British Library.

A catalog record for this book is available from the Library of Congress.

ISSN 1479-344X

ISBN 978-0-2415-6897-2

Printed and bound in China

www.dk.com

As a guide to abbreviations in visitor information blocks: **Adm** = admission charge; **D** = dinner; **L** = lunch.

MIX
Paper from responsible sources
FSC™ C018179
www.fsc.org

This book was made with Forest Stewardship Council ™ certified paper – one small step in DK's commitment to a sustainable future. For more information go to www.dk.com/our-green-pledge

Phrase Book

Thai is a tonal language and regarded by most linguists as head of a distinct language group, though it incorporates many Sanskrit words from ancient India, and some modern English ones, too. There are five tones: mid, high, low, rising, and falling. The particular tone, or pitch, at which each syllable is pronounced determines its meaning. For instance "mài" (falling tone) means "not," but "mǎi" (rising tone) is "silk." See the Guidelines for Pronunciation, below, for a phonetic transliteration of the Thai script for English speakers, including guidance for tones in the form of accents.

Guidelines for Pronunciation

When reading the phonetics, pronounce syllables as if they form English words. For instance:

a = as in "*a*go"	*ay* = as in "d*ay*"
e = as in "h*e*n"	*er* = as in "ent*er*"
i = as in "th*i*n"	*ew* = as in "f*ew*"
o = as in "*o*n"	*oh* = as in "g*o*"
u = as in "g*u*n"	*oo* = as in "b*oo*t"
ah = as in "r*a*ther"	*OO* = as in "b*oo*k"
ai = as in "Th*ai*"	*oy* = as in "t*oy*"
air = as in "p*air*"	*g* = as in "*g*ive"
ao = as in "M*ao* Zedong"	*ng* = as in "si*ng*"

These sounds have no close equivalents in English:

eu	can be likened to a sound of disgust - the sound could be written as "errgh"
bp	a single sound between a "b" and a "p"
dt	a single sound between a "d" and a "t"

Note that when "p," "t," and "k" occur at the end of Thai words, the sound is "swallowed." Also note that many Thais use an "l" instead of an "r" sound.

The Five Tones

Accents indicate the tone of each syllable.

no mark	The *mid tone* is voiced at the speaker's normal, even pitch.	
á é í ó ú	The *high tone* is pitched slightly higher than the mid tone.	
à è ì ò ù	The *low tone* is pitched slightly lower than the mid tone.	
ǎ ě ǐ ǒ ǔ	The *rising tone* sounds like a questioning pitch, starting low and rising.	
â ê î ô û	The *falling tone* sounds similar to a syllable word for emphasis.	

In an Emergency

Help!	*chôo-ay dôo-ay!*
Fire!	*fai mài!*
Where is the nearest hospital?	*tǎir-o-née mee rohng pa-yah-bahn yòo têe-nǎi?*
Call an ambulance!	*rêe-uk rót pa-yah-bahn hâi nòy!*
Call a doctor!	*rêe-uk mǒr hâi nòy!*
Call the police!	*rêe-uk dtum ròo-ut hâi nòy!*

Communication Essentials

Yes	*châi or krúp/kà*
No	*mâi châi or mâi krúp/mâi kâ*

Please can you...?	*chôo-ay*
Thank you	*kòrp-kOOn*
No, thank you	*mâi ao kòrp-kOOn*
Excuse me/sorry	*kǒr-tôht (krúp/kà)*
Hello	*sa-wùt dee (krúp/kà)*
Goodbye	*lah gòrn ná*

Useful Phrases

How are you?	*kOOn sa-bai dee reu (krúp/kà)?*
Very well, thank you	*sa-bai dee (krúp/kà)*
How do I get to...?	*...bpai yung-ngai?*
Do you speak English?	*kOOn pôot pah-sǎh ung-grit bpen mái?*
I can't speak Thai.	*pôot pah-sǎh tai mâi bpen*
Where is the nearest public telephone?	*tǎir-o née mee toh-ra-sùp yòo têe-nǎi?*

Useful Words

hot	*rórn*
cold	*yen or nǎo*
good	*dee*
bad	*mâi dee*
open	*bpèrt*
closed	*bpìt*
left	*sái*
right	*kwǎh*
near	*glâi*
toilet	*hôrng náhm*

Shopping

How much does this cost?	*nêe rah-kah tâo-rài?*
Do you have?	*mee...mái?*
Do you take credit cards/traveler's checks?	*rub but cray-dìt/ chék dern tang mái?*
What time do you open/close?	*bpèrt/bpìt gèe mohng?*
Can you ship this overseas?	*sóng khǒng nee bpai dtàhng bpra-tâyt*
Could you lower the price a bit?	*dâi mái? lót rah-kah nòy dâi mái?*
How about...baht?	*...bàht dâi mái?*
I'll settle for...baht.	*...bàht gôr láir-o-gun*
Thai silk	*pâh-mǎi tai*
pharmacy	*ráhn kǎi yah*
market	*dta-làht*
supermarket	*sÓOp-bpêr-mah-gêt*

Staying in a Hotel

Do you have a vacant room?	*mee hôrng wâhng mái?*
air-conditioned room	*hôrng air*
I'd like a room for one night/ three nights.	*(pôm/dee-chún) ja pùk yòo keun nèung/ sǎhm keun*

What is the charge per night? — *kâh hôrng wun la tâo-rái?*
May I see the room first please? — *kŏr doo hôrng gòrn dâi mái?*
Will you spray some mosquito repellent, please? — *chôo-ay chèet yah gun yOOng hâi nòy dâi mái?*
double/twin room — *hôrng kôo*
single room — *hôrng dèe-o*
bill — *bin*
key — *gOOn-jair*
shower — *fùk boo-a*
swimming pool — *sá wâi náhm*

Sightseeing

tourist office — *sŭm-núk ngahn gahn tôrng têe-o*
tourist police — *dtum-ròo-ut tôrng têe-o*
beach — *háht or chai-háht*
island (ko) — *gòr*
museum — *pí-pít-ta-pun*
national park — *ÒO-ta yahn háirng châht*
temple (wat) — *wút*
Thai boxing — *moo-ay tai*
Thai massage — *nôo-ut*
trekking — *gahn dern tahng táo*

Transportation

How long does it take to get to...? — *chái way-lah nahn tâo-rài bpai tĕung têe...?*
What station is this? — *têe nêe sa-tăhn-nee a-rai?*
ticket — *dtŏo-a*
air-conditioned bus — *rót bprùp ah-gàht*
airport — *sa-năhm bin*
tour bus — *rót too-a*
train — *rót fai*
bus station — *sa-tăhn-nee rót may*
moped — *rót mor-dter-sai*
taxi — *táirk-sêe*

Eating Out

A table for two please. — *kŏr dtó sŭm-rùp sŏrng kon*
May I see the menu? — *kŏr doo may-noo nòy?*
Do you have...? — *mee...mái?*
Is it spicy? — *pèt mái?*
May I have a glass of water, please. — *kŏr núm kăirng bplào gâir-o nèung*
Waiter/waitress! — *kOOn (krúp/kâ)*
The check, please. — *kŏr bin nòy (krúp/kâ)*

Menu Decoder

néu-a woo-a — beef
bee-a — beer
yâhng — char-grilled
gài — chicken
prík — chili
gah-fair — coffee
bpoo — crab
mèe gròrp — crispy noodles
gŏo-ay dtĕe-o hâirng — dry noodles
bpèt — duck
tÓO-ree-un — durian
kài — egg
bplah — fish
kĭng — ginger
núm kăirng bplào — iced water
hèt — mushroom
gŏo-ay dtĕe-o-náhm — noodle soup
ma-la-gor — papaya
sùp-bpa-rót — pineapple
néu-a-mŏo — pork
kâo — rice
gŏo-ay dtĕe-o — rice noodles
gÔOng — shrimp
ah-hăhn wăhng — soy sauce
núm chah — tea
pùk — vegetables
náhm — water

Health

I do not feel well — *róâ-sèuk mâi sa-bai*
I have a fever — *dtoo-a-rórn bpen kâi*
asthma — *rôhk hèut*
diabetes — *rôhk bao wăhn*
diarrhea — *tórng sĕe-a*
dizzy — *wee-un hŏo-a*
stomach ache — *bpòo-ut tórng*
aspirin — *air-sa-bprin or yah-gâir kâi*
doctor — *mŏr*
dentist — *tun-dta-pâirt or mŏr fun*
hospital — *rohng pa-yah-bahn*
medicine — *yah*
prescription — *bai sùng yah*
I'm allergic to... — *(pŏm/dee-chún) páir...*

Numbers

0 — *sŏon*
1 — *nèung*
2 — *sŏrng*
3 — *săhm*
4 — *sèe*
5 — *hâh*
6 — *hòk*
7 — *jèt*
8 — *bpàirt*
9 — *gâo*
10 — *sìp*
100 — *nèung róy*
1000 — *nèung pan*
one hour — *nèung chôo-a mohng*
half an hour — *krêung chôo-a mohng*
Sunday — *wun ah-tít*
Monday — *wun jun*
Tuesday — *wun ung-kahn*
Wednesday — *wun pÓOt*
Thursday — *wun pa-réu-hùt*
Friday — *wun sÒOk*
Saturday — *wun săo*

Selected Sight Index